And Prevent

How to Get Rid of
Swimming Pool Algae
by rudy stankowitz

This one is dedicated to all of the folks that maintain swimming pools for a living. The water warriors out at the break of day and sometimes earlier, the men and women that bust tail to ensure backyard and public swimming pools are safe, healthy, and everything that a bather wants it to be.

ISBN: 9798702035543
Imprint: Independently published

Printed in the United States of America.
First printing edition 2021.
Copyright © 2021 Rudy Stankowitz.

Printed in the United States of America.
First printing edition 2019.

Author page www.rudystankowitz.com

Aquatic Education & Consulting www,CPOclass.com

Edit & Fact check by

Richard A. Falk Consulting

Isaac Miller, Ph.D. Microbiology, algal physiology and community ecology in aquatic systems

Contents

Introduction

Hey guys, this is Rudy. Thank you, and welcome you to the *How to Get Rid of* Swimming Pool Algae *Handbook.* I know, super original name, but I believe in calling it what it is.

In this handbook, we will cover the best methods of algae prevention, algae identification, and of course, the best steps on getting rid of the stuff. When finished, we will have covered the methods and precautions necessary to keep run-ins with Al G. Bloom to a bare minimum. About as much protection as you could have just shy of a mini-forcefield around the pool.

Why put it all in a book? Honestly, I don't see a reason why anyone should have to reinvent the wheel. I've been doing this for a very long time; I care about this industry's future and swimming pools' health and safety. I like the idea of continually making the swimming pool world better by paying it forward, so I thought I could share some things that I have picked up along the way; my swimming pool algae triumphs and tribulations. So, I'm hoping you pick up some tidbits in these pages that you can use to make your swimming pools safer, easier to maintain, and your company more profitable.

I have also made some pretty cool discoveries in some field studies, and I wanted to share those with you. If you are looking at algae differently by the time you've finished reading, mainly black algae, that is just a part of what I hope to accomplish (insert evil scientist laugh here). Always remember the rules of engagement: ensure a sufficient supply of caffeine, and know your enemy.

Yes, I know, there are already quite a few great books available on pool care written by some of the industry's top minds. I don't see any reason to clutter that market, but I want to write some stuff down before getting too much older, and I start to forget. Lol. That said, I have decided to go a very topic-specific route. Instead of a general familiarization on A-to-Z pool care, this handbook is all about being an *Algae Prevention and Eradication Specialist*.

I have also created an online Certification course that compliments this handbook, which will validate your commitment to skills, knowledge, and proficiency on the topic, providing you with a marketable point of difference that will give you an edge over your competition.

Let's face it; the chances are that anyone who takes care of swimming pools will have a run-in with the Big Green Monster at some point in time. That's a good part of the reason I chose Algae. It is also one of the areas where all of the cogs need to be in place. It's not just chemistry; algae prevention and eradication involve circulation, filtration, and even an awareness of the environment. I don't want to delve too deeply into those regular maintenance practices; however, I will discuss the value of each in both prevention and eradication of algae.

Note: It is much easier to prevent algae than it is to get rid of it.

Think outside the pool

Who is the better maintenance person? The maintenance tech who locates the trip hazard before it becomes an issue. Or, the maintenance tech who repairs the trip hazard really fast after someone face plants?

Prevention can only truly work if we can figure out what we need to prevent. Yes, a pool is a pool, and water is water. However, most factors that lead to algae growth are environmental, so we would be mashugana if we didn't consider the environment in determining a treatment plan. That is unless your goal is to 'Splash 'N Dash' your way through pool care, and your customer development method involves a 'Turn 'em and Burn 'em' philosophy. We laugh, but we all know a competitor who does just that, and I often wonder how they manage to stay in business. If this is you, the 'Dump and Run' pool tech, then me and my book are probably going to annoy you.

"Think outside the box." is a viral expression from the 60s but came to its own in the 1990s. Everything was "Think outside the box." Everyone searched for "Out of the box" thinkers if you looked through the help wanted ads. Every applicant to every interviewer, "I think outside the box." Think outside the box, crush the box, burn the box, destroy the box, everything was about the box. I just want to suggest the same train of thought; after all, isn't a swimming pool just a box filled with water?

'Think outside the pool' has become my mantra

Look at each swimming pool as an individual, unique as a fingerprint with environmental and human factors specific to that one backyard oasis or aquatic facility. Here's the thing, there are no cookie-cutter pools with cookie-cutter chemical needs. They don't exist; it may be yard conditions, tree canopy, or even proximity to a natural body of water that makes a pool unrepeatable in care protocol. We need to identify each of these things and more. The goal is to be able to head off a problem before it becomes a problem.

When you are at a property for the first time, you should make a habit of looking up, down, left, and right. Everything you see is telling a story of what to expect. A planter close to a pool edge usually results in mustard algae as it is inevitable that it will overflow potting soil into the pool during heavy rain (It doesn't take much. 1000 ppb phosphate in an 18,000-gallon pool is only 2.4 ounces weight of phosphate or 1.4 ounces weight of 0-45-0 fertilizer (45% by weight of P_2O_5). If the pool is close to a natural body of water, we are close to the source - algae spores are airborne, and a short distance to a pond means the spores don't have as far to travel. A pool on a golf

course can be a phosphate nightmare. Pine trees as part of a canopy overhead will result in a consistently low pH.

A dog that swims in a pool will significantly affect the water's chlorine demand and maintenance (how much, of course, depends on the dog). Note everything from unkempt lawns to red cedar much. These things are unique to each property and control the pool's water quality/chemistry. The key is to find a way to work with these variables, not fight them. Although we may have some influence on human factors, going fisticuffs with Mother nature is a never-ending scrap we cannot win. In embracing the science in what we do, pool care becomes super easy.

Parts per million per billion

Are we clear on what a ppb (part per billion) is? A ppm (part per million)? Just in case, I want to get this taken care of right off the bat because I will use this repeatedly throughout this handbook and in the certification class. My plan here is to keep my technobabble to a minimum.

If I hit the lotto and win one billion dollars and then give you one hundred dollars out of my winnings, that would be 100 ppb. Parts per million is similar, except instead of a billionaire; I am only a millionaire (I won't complain either way). I've heard some compare a gallon of water to a 1M gallon pool, but that is not entirely accurate unless that gallon came from the pool, leaving 999,999 gallons behind.

Consider your customer

If you can identify a problem before it becomes a problem, you can have a conversation with that customer explaining what you have found and the likely outcome. For example, screen-enclosed pools in Florida are trendy. These do a fantastic job of keeping leaves and debris out of the pool, but they are not without their own maintenance needs.

Screen enclosures should have a professional cleaning at least once, preferably twice a year. If not, they can become problematic. Have you ever seen a dirty screen? They get that ominous green tint to them, and then up overhead, leaves, twigs, and pine needles collect. It's no secret that we don't get near as much rain in the colder months as we do in the summer, so throughout the winter, these leaves and screen algae become drier than a stick of beef jerky.

 Did you ever make yourself a cup of hot tea? Place the bag in hot water, and after a moment, you can see the tea cascading from the packet. Isn't a tea bag just dried leaves on a screen? The same thing we have overhead. Then March comes along, and we get that first torrential downpour of the season. The debris on top of the enclosure becomes saturated, just like the teabag, and drips directly into the pool. When this occurs, you will see an increase in phosphates. How much of a problem this is for you will vary from pool to pool as it is dependent on the amount and plant material type the screen collects.

If you explain the importance of screen cleaning to the customer before the pool becomes challenging to maintain, you have put the ball into their court, whether they have it cleaned or not. Then when it turns, you can remind them of your warning. In this scenario, this lack of maintenance is the customer's fault. If you wait until after it turns green to point out that the screens have needed cleaning for six or seven months, all your customer is hearing is an excuse. Communication before the fact will make your life a tremendous amount easier.

An Ounce of Prevention

This is so simple; we may just have never thought it would work. However, after water chemistry and filtration, brushing the pool walls and floor with a nylon bristle brush regularly is your best defense against algae. Yes, brushing! This is probably one of the first steps omitted when strapped for time, but please don't skip it. Brushing will only get easier to ignore after you let it slide the first time. From here, the potential to become a bad habit increases exponentially. Trust me; I get it. Unless there is visible algae growth on the walls, there is no immediate reward. Still, you can soon come to regret this 'To brush. Or, not to brush' decision.

Pro Tip: Try wearing polarized sunglasses. You will be able to see the beginnings of algae before visible to the homeowner or property manager; let's call it a 'Final Warning.' But don't wear the shades when conducting your water test. Polarized glasses will make the colors you are trying to match look all farkakte.

When I say 'Embrace the science in what we do,' this is not me saying go out and buy every chemical available and dump them in. No, no, no! Science encompasses many things. Remember to 'Think outside the Pool.' This goes way beyond the water, but the water is indeed included. We need to continually find ways to work with what mother nature is giving us. Work with the hand we are dealt.

Brushing helps us to gain the upper hand on algae. Remember that these little suckers are microscopic and unseen to the human eye until there are thousands, if not more, invading the pool(s) you maintain. Just because you can't see it, it doesn't mean that it isn't there. Brushing dislodges algae, removes protective coatings, allows the chlorine more area to attack, and permits your filter to collect what it can.

Not Algae, this is a copper problem

Algae are always present whether you see them or not

How often should we brush? The answer to that is as often as you can. Many commercial pools implement this as part of their daily routine, and for good reason; it works! Still, I know that this is not always possible due to work schedules and, well, just life; if you can hit the walls and the floor of a residential pool once a week, that would be ideal. Even once every two weeks is helpful. A brushing schedule of any less than that, and you'll risk allowing algae to take hold, in particular black algae (which we will discuss in the sections ahead).

Don't forget the disinfectant

Maintaining a high active chlorine level is vital in algae prevention. Hence, a minimum chlorine level of 7.5% free chlorine to cyanuric acid (i.e., CyA of 50ppm to FC of 3.75 ppm) is necessary if we are NOT monitoring phosphate levels. If you keep tabs on the 'phos' and are less than 500 ppb, a 1.0 ppm minimum FC, when a CYA of 0 to 50 ppm exists, is all you need providing the key factors we discuss in the following pages are part of your protocol of care.

For residential pool service, this works right into the routine. I was never comfortable with less than three visits each week for a commercial pool when I had my service company, but again that's just me. I've made two trips per week begrudgingly but would outright refuse a one-time per week public pool customer. At that point, I believe they are only using me for my certification/license. That's a hard NO!

Automation is essential in commercial pools and is a strong suggestion for residential for these same reasons. Without it, a chlorine demand will quickly use up what you have, and the algae will grow faster than it can kill it. Of course, if we are using trichlor, you'll have to monitor the rising cyanuric acid level (discussed in sections ahead).

1909 portable emergency hypochlorite device. CDC/ Minnesota Department of Health, R.N. Barr Library; Librarians Melissa Rethlefsen and Marie Jones.

Water Chemistry

Get yourself a good quality test kit. It doesn't need to be ridiculously expensive, but it should be accurate and have the ability to test more than just chlorine and pH. I prefer we steer clear of the two bottle and five bottle test kits that you see online that use the chemical OTO (orthotolidine) for testing chlorine. These are not the right test kits for you unless you plan to bring water samples to the pool store every week. The chemical OTO cannot differentiate between Free Chlorine and Total Chlorine, so you would never know how much of the chlorine in the water is working like it should and how much is not. This inability is why regulations do not allow the two and five bottle test kits for commercial pool use.

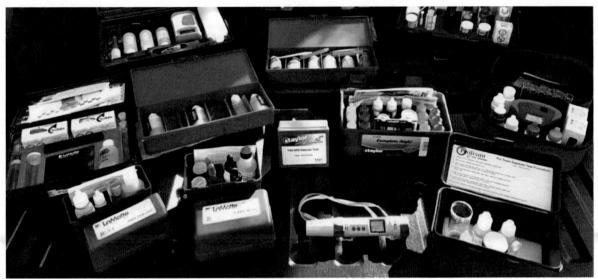
A few from my collection

You need to pick up a test kit that can test for all essential pool water values. We need a test kit that can differentiate between Free Chlorine and Total Chlorine; otherwise, you will never really know when you need to shock the pool. Yes!!! The 'third yellow bottle' is part of the two-part test that will determine if a combined chlorine level exists, which, if it does, is the reason we shock a pool. This bottle, DPD 3, is usually pretty easy to locate in most test kits because it is the one that is still full.

Our kit should contain a means of testing Free Chlorine, Total Chlorine, pH, Total Alkalinity, Calcium Hardness, and Cyanuric Acid (if we are using it). This is at a minimum. You should honestly own a means of testing for everything you put into the water for which a test kit exists. Keep in mind that it will be easier to determine the level of combined chlorine using either a FAS-DPD titration (count the drops) or photometer than with a DPD drop test. These methods of testing will also give you greater control over your chlorine chemistry in general.

Everything starts with an analysis

A couple of months back, I had tripped over a tchotchke that had mysteriously appeared on the floor and then ass over elbow into a laundry basket. With a limp and a bruised tuchus, I hobbled my way to the nearest doc in a box. Guess what? Before permitted to see an MD, they sent me to this magical place known a triage. You got it! The doctors would not see me until they received the test results.

The Nurse also asked me to get up onto the scale. The medical staff wanted to know precisely how much of me the physician would be dealing with before we could go any further—the same holds true with the pool's gallonage. If we do not know how much water we have, how could we ever size equipment or calculate chemical doses accurately? BTW - I am at that age now where the Doctor's office scale serves as a not so gentle reminder to lay off the Carrot cake.

Langelier Saturation Index

I know many would tell you that water balance doesn't matter when it comes to algae. However, this is pretty far from the truth. Of course, it matters. I don't plan on getting into the mathematical calculations here, just a few words on why we should care about LSI (Langelier Saturation Index) in algae treatment prevention.

We know the Langelier Saturation Index is used to determine water balance, and we understand that this calculation pertains only to the safety of the vessel. We use it to prevent possible plaster damage. The water is either corrosive, scale forming, or neither (neither is the goal). This would lead one to believe the index would not affect algae. I know, I'm letting my 'Sybil' show.

However, if the water should be out of balance and aggressive for some time, it will etch the plaster. The etching will create tiny dead spots in circulation where algae may find a foothold. Try picturing all the nooks and crannies of an English muffin.

This, of course, is a Cliff Notes version. Sticking with the theme of making a swimming pool easier to take care of, I will tell you that you do not need a bunch of tricky math here. There are many great apps available on the market today for LSI calculation. Heck, you may even find that your chemical test kit has come with a manual slide for such computation. If you decide to get an app, try to find one that doesn't try to sell you stuff beyond pH, Total Alkalinity, and Calcium Hardness adjusters. These are the only needs that an LSI calculation can determine.

Yes, this is important in both vinyl and fiberglass pools. See the upcoming section on calcium hardness.

People ask me all the time if pool professionals calculate the saturation index at the pools they maintain. My answer is always the same. "The pool pros that make a lot of money do." First, there is a considerable risk to the pool, as discussed above, if they don't. Secondly, people usually don't mind spending more if the expense is justified, and they believe that they are getting their money's worth. So, do things the right way and then increase your rates by 10%.

Interestingly, the Langelier Saturation Index is a simplified version of the Calcium Saturation Index (CSI) created back in 1936 by Dr. Wilfred Langelier. Many years after its conception, the CSI, which many still use, was altered, allowing for ease in the manual calculation and then named for the doctor. With that, I find it surprising that so many develop apps designed to calculate the less accurate LSI while the technology could easily support a more precise computation.

Ideal Range

Okeydokey, now. It is essential to know what you are shooting for when testing the water, and this is it. Yes, I did put a date in the top left corner of the chart. The reason for the date is in anticipating change. These are my suggested levels, and I know they all may not be what you are used to, but there is a reason for my madness. I expect a change in the maximum acceptable chlorine level to come from the CMAHC (Committee for the Model Aquatic Health Code) shortly, and four ppm will likely be the magic number. My reasoning for my suggested ideal level of 30 ppm for CyA is explained in my comments on the CDC Fecal Incident Response Recommendation below the chart.

You'll find that your local health department tends to rely heavily on the MAHC suggested mins, maxes, and ideals. Those regulations in your health department's public pool code are the only ones that matter if you are maintaining commercial bodies of water. Residential pools should adhere to the same ranges even though they are not regulated. Look at it as a strong suggestion. You don't have to when dealing with a backyard pool, but you should. If not spot on with the DOH (Dept. of Health) are pretty darn close, I think you'll find my numbers. The maximum chlorine level is a federal law

	Acceptable Range	Ideal Range
Free Chlorine (DPD-FC)	1.0 ppm - 4.0 ppm	FC as a % to CyA 1.0 ppm - 4.0 ppm w/o CyA
Combined Chlorine level	< 0.2 ppm	0 ppm
pH	7.2 - 7.8	7.4 - 7.6
Total Alkalinity	60 ppm - 180 ppm	80 ppm - 100 ppm
Calcium Hardness	150 ppm - 1,000 ppm	200 ppm - 400 ppm
Cyanuric Acid (CyA) Residential	< 90 ppm (w/o use of dilution test) < 180 ppm (w/ dilution test where approved)	30 - 50 ppm
Cyanuric Acid (CyA) Commercial	< 90 ppm (w/o use of dilution test) < 180 ppm (w/ dilution test where approved)	< 30 ppm*
Total Dissolved Solids	< 1,500 ppm (excludes saltwater pools)	Same as Acceptable
Borates	< 50 ppm	30 - 50 ppm

*The CDC's 2018 Fecal Incident Response Recommendations for Aquatic Staff states that in handling a diarrheal incident in water with CyA present, one must drop the cyanuric acid level to below 15 ppm before beginning treatment. If a level of 30 ppm is maintained, the initial step in the process would involve replacing half of the water. A higher level of CyA would require draining more than half the pool.

A maximum acceptable level of 180 ppm CyA would depend upon the operator's demonstrated proficiency in using a dilution test and only where approved by the regulating authority.

pH

pH is the negative base-ten logarithm of Hydrogen ion activity. It is easiest explained as the measure of the water's 'Need' for acid. If the pH is high, we 'Need' acid. If the pH is low, we don't 'Need' acid. This is not to be confused with acid 'demand,' which would refer to the required dose, and that would be dependent on pH buffering, mostly Total Alkalinity.

Power of Hydrogen, Potential of Hydrogen, or Potenz Hydrogen? In Copenhagen, the Carlsberg Laboratory insists the initials stand for "Power of Hydrogen." This is where Soren Sorensen created the scale, and this will be the definition of the acronym we use.

The pH scale runs from 0 to 14, which leads us to believe that '0' would be as acidic as something can be, and 14 is as base as base gets. However, in actuality, this is NOT a closed scale. For example, Muriatic Acid (31.45% HCl) has a pH of -1, which, of course, is less than '0'. This does not change the fact that 7.0 is neutral and that we in the pool industry only deal with a wee portion of this scale. As I am sure you are already aware, pool water has an acceptable pH range of 7.2 to 7.8. There are, of course, reasons we shoot for this.

Understand that there are really only two things that use up chlorine – UV degradation from the sunlight. The Second is chlorine itself - Chlorine uses itself up as it sanitizes and disinfects. We are also aware that the rate of disinfection is pH-dependent; the lower the pH, the more effective the chlorine. This would suggest that we burn through chlorine quicker at a low pH; however, this is only true if there is something in the water for the chlorine to react with. With that said, you can achieve an equivalent FAC level at a higher pH by merely increasing the amount of chlorine.

We shoot for a pH of 7.5, the ideal range being 7.4 to 7.6. I know you already know that a low pH is corrosive and has the potential to damage both the pool and its equipment. I am sure you are aware we don't want the pH to be too high, either. We will lose more chlorine at a high pH than when it is low, especially when cyanuric acid is present. This occurs because the CyA tries to keep the HOCl (hypochlorous acid) constant as the pH rises, which results in a rapidly increasing OCl^-, (hypochlorite), which breaks down in sunlight much more quickly than HOCl.

We can also manage the 'algae killing power' of chlorine at a higher pH by slightly increasing the pool's chlorine level. It doesn't take much. An amount just 15% higher will give you the same HOCl at a pH of 8.0 that you would see at 7.5.

Can a high pH cause cloudy water?

Yes, absolutely. But, not for the reasons you may be thinking. The impact of pH on water clarity is directly due to its role in the saturation index. The higher the saturation index, the cloudier it will become due to an over-saturation of calcium carbonate. This, of course, means that we can easily maintain the water's clarity in a swimming pool with a high pH, providing that we account for the contribution of pH to that index by maintaining a lower Calcium Hardness and Total Alkalinity.

Total Alkalinity

Total Alkalinity is the measure of carbonates, bicarbonates, cyanurate ions, and hydroxides. It has much to do with the water's pH level, or at least how long it stays in place and how far it moves when it does. The Total Alkalinity does not change as quickly as pH, so it doesn't need frequent testing. Unless, of course, we are talking about a residential weekly service account. In that case, we would test during each visit. Otherwise, two to three times per week is more than adequate. Because we cannot adjust the pH without affecting the Total Alkalinity (excluding aeration), it would be a good idea to check after a pH adjustment in either direction.

Bicarbonate ion

TA (Total Alkalinity) is not a test we should ever altogether skip; after all, it is the water's ability to resist a change in pH. Sometimes we also refer to the Total Alkalinity as the buffering capacity of water. It "deadens" the impact of things like rain, pine needles, or your method of chlorination (trichlor or dichlor) that can drive your pH downward. Without a decent TA level, the pH would bounce a bit about the scale.

I know we learn that dichlor (Sodium dichloro-s-triazinetrione) is neutral as far as pH is concerned, but that is not entirely true. The product does have a pH close to 7.0. But, chlorine getting used up is an acidic process, giving us an acidic net result.

To me, it seems like any other way would be a significant pain in the patootie. Why test and adjust, then test and adjust, only to test and adjust again. I'm sure you have better things to do than to babysit the pH. Let the Total Alkalinity be the babysitter of pH for you. Sure, we still need to check in from time to time, but we can do so, knowing that everything is likely to be found to be okay. Or, at least pretty freaking close.

The pH scale is logarithmic, so think in multiples of 10. A pH of 6.0 is 10x more acidic than a pH of 7.0 but 100x more acidic than a pH of 8.0. The greater the distance our pH is from where we want it to be, the more chemical it will take to get there, exponentially.

Total Alkalinity, on the other hand, is linear. The same dose in the same amount of water will always give us the same result: 1.4 lbs of sodium bicarbonate in 10K gallons of water will provide us with an increase of 10 ppm.

The Total Alkalinity/pH Relationship

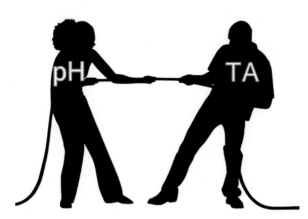

Perhaps the easiest way to view the two is that pH is the measurement of the water's need for acid, and Total Alkalinity is a buffer (The water's ability to resist a change in pH). Yes, the acid will lower both pH and Total Alkalinity no matter how you add it. Soda ash will increase both pH and TA a substantial amount. Sodium bicarbonate will generate a significant increase in Total Alkalinity but only a slight increase in pH. This makes bicarb the better choice when we need to increase the TA, but the pH is acceptable.

One pound of soda ash in 10K gallons of water will raise the TA by 11.3 ppm. One pound of baking soda in 10K gallons of water will increase the TA by 7.1 ppm.

When the pH is low, we add soda ash. If we have a low Total Alkalinity, we add sodium bicarbonate. It's a hammer and nail scenario. Baking soda (sodium bicarbonate) has a low pH of 8.4, so it will take much more of the product to see a minimal increase in pH at the pH range we typically maintain in swimming pools. However, if the Total Alkalinity is in the ideal range, the pH will usually find its way home on its own.

Unfortunately, using bicarb to adjust pH because soda ash clouds the water will skyrocket the Total Alkalinity if we are not careful. This, in turn, will create the need to add acid to lower Total Alkalinity, which also lowers pH, and we get stuck in a never-ending yo-yo of pool care frustration.

The Better Business Bureau

While we are on the subject of Total Alkalinity, I have a story that I wasn't sure I should share here, but I think it's funny, so why not. This is about the only BBB complaint I had ever received.

This goes way back to the mid-nineties. I was a manager of a retail swimming pool supply store on Long Island. Of course, computers weren't a big thing yet; I'm pretty sure I didn't even own one at the time. I get a letter from the Better Business Bureau that somebody had filed a complaint, and the BBB wanted me to respond. This is pretty much verbatim to what the customer complaint read (I don't think I will ever forget).

"Either Rudy does not know what he is doing, or he is perpetuating a scam. I took my water sample into XYZ Pool Supplies, where Rudy tested it and then told me which items I needed to purchase to 'correct' my water chemistry. Mr. Stankowitz stated that I needed twenty-five pounds of Alkalinity Increaser because my Total Alkalinity was low. I have never had to add this Alkalinity Increaser before, so I just took my water bottle and left."

"Later that night, I added fifteen pounds of baking soda like I do every year after opening my pool. The next day I took a water sample to a different pool store. It turns out I only needed ten pounds of the Alkalinity Increaser. Rudy was trying to rip me off."

I'm just going to leave this here. I am sure I don't have to explain the humor in the complaint. Of course, Total Alkalinity Increaser is just a big ole tub of baking soda.

Calcium Hardness

Calcium is very different than a lot of other things we deal with when maintaining swimming pools. Water is a universal solvent, which is kind of true but not really because there are some things that water can't dissolve. Let's say a liquefier to most, but especially those that form ions in water, like calcium and carbonate. What is the nearest source of calcium for the water in your pool? If you said the pool plaster, then we are on the same page. If you answered "the bones of people swimming," just know that I am somewhere shaking my head - I've lost count of the number of times that I am given this as the answer to that question. The dissolvent quality of H_2O is why we must saturate the water with both calcium and carbonate; attempting to do this with one or the other, or not at all, is when damage, known as etching, occurs.

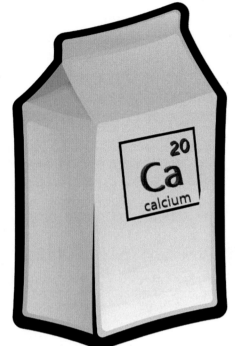

You don't deal with plaster pools? We still should be concerned about Calcium Hardness (CH). Fiberglass swimming pools with soft water are known to be more prone to cobalt staining than those with a higher calcium level. Yes, the real cause is pinholes in the gelcoat. However, cobalt staining tends to be more visible when the CH level is low.

The vinyl used to manufacture liners for swimming pools often contains calcium carbonate. There is some evidence of undersaturated water pulling calcium carbonate from vinyl when the content of such is higher than 7%. Still, I don't believe anyone has studied the long-term effect as of yet.

Too much calcium is not a good thing either. We shoot for a 200 ppm level to 400 ppm, though in high water hardness areas, we counter the potentially negative impact of a tremendous amount of calcium by keeping a lower pH and TA (Total Alkalinity). If the saturation index is too high, it could lead to cloudy water or even deposits on the tile and the plaster. This is known as scale. These deposits can sometimes be a real Mother Father to get rid of, so it is best to monitor the LSI to avoid this scale build-up from occurring in the first place. We will address this later, but I wanted to mention here that mustard algae need a higher calcium level to thrive, which is another reason we need to keep tabs on our calcium.

Please keep in the front of your noodle that the only way we can lower the calcium hardness level is by replacing water, some or all. We also need first to make sure this drain and fill will be worthwhile. Test the Calcium Hardness (CH) level of the fill water first. If we see that the amount here is 500 ppm, and the pool's measure is 500 ppm - a drain and fill will change everything except the CH. That'll poop in your corn flakes?

Because we are concerned with Calcium Hardness and not Total Hardness, we will have to rule out test strips as a means of measure. A test strip can only read Total Hardness, including any magnesium (Mg) in the sample. This can be significant. Depending upon your water source, Mg can account for as much as twenty-five percent of your test result, in some areas, even higher.

NOTE: You should only drain water if you are a properly insured and licensed (if required) swimming pool professional with an awareness of groundwater tables and knowledge in the installation of well-points.

Borates

We discussed how Total Alkalinity buffers best against a downward drift in pH. It's only fair we talk about increasing our ability to buffer against an upward rise. Establishing a borate level in the water can help you do this. Here we get a little sciencey, but to understand how this works, we need to talk pK_a. This, pK_a, is the negative logarithm of the acid dissociation constant. WTF does that mean??? This is all about the giving and taking of protons.

If the pH is lower than the acid's pKa value, it will be more difficult for the pH to rise. So, we say we are buffering against an upward drift. "Buffering better" against an upward drift would be a more appropriate statement because the benefit will be in both directions. If the pK_a value is lower than the pH, then it becomes more difficult to lower. Here we say we are buffering against a downward drift. By understanding pK_a values, we can kinda sorta almost but not really lock our pH in place. Okay, back to borates.

The pK_a value of boric acid is 9.2, and from here, we look one up and one down, which means that we will have our most enormous buffering capacity at a pH from 8.2 to 10.2. Imagine riding a bicycle down the highway, and the road is perfectly flat, with no hills, zero grade. We are just zooming along with little effort passing mile markers with ease.

We peddle past 5.2, then 6.2, and still have yet to break a sweat. From 6.0 to 7.0, no problem. But from mile marker 7.2 to 8.2, we hit a pretty decent incline requiring much more effort to go the same distance than the mile before. Then from mile marker 8.2 to 9.2, Fuhgeddaboudit, we're practically heading straight up the hill.

The same is true of Total Alkalinity (bicarbonate buffering system) in preventing a downward drift in pH due to a 6.1 pK_a value. Remember one up, one down? Thus, Total Alkalinity having its highest buffering capacity between a 5.1 to 7.1 pH. This is why the Borate/Total Alkalinity combo works well at buffering pH at the typical levels used in pool care, an acceptable pH range of 7.2 to 7.8.

You see, we do not really "lock" the pH in place; with the use of buffers, we are just making it a lot harder for it to move. Do keep in mind that an acid's pKa value will go down if the salt level should increase. Ahem, ahem, saltwater pools.

Wait, why the big deal about buffers? Remember earlier, when we spoke of the effect of pH on the Langelier Saturation Index? This value will make significant changes to the LSI with minor movement. Having a little help to prevent a climbing pH is never a bad thing, but keep in mind that borates will also contribute slightly to the saturation index. We also mentioned earlier that a higher pH would result in more significant chlorine loss due to solar UV degradation and less effective chlorine (unless we add more chlorine).

Besides preventing an upward drift in pH, a borate level in the water will provide some extra protection from UV degradation and serve as an algastat. This means that it will aid in preventing algae growth. It won't kill it, but it will help to keep it away.

Please remember that borates in water do not degrade. Much like a high Calcium or Cyanuric Acid level, we will need to have a pool professional replace water to lower those levels if they get too high.

You might find that you need to top off occasionally due to loss of borates from backwashing, bather drag out, or bather splash-out. This, in everyday use, will not occur that frequently, though the amount of water expelled during the backwash of a commercial pool filter will expedite loss.

I only stress this because if you dose too high, draining is the solution. This is part of why I DO NOT recommend using Borax to raise pH (Boric acid can also establish a borate residual without an increase in pH). Even though the chemical in Borax (disodium tetraborate) will get the job done, bear in mind that frequent additions will steadily increase the borate level. This will eventually get to a point where water replacement is the only option for correction.

The ideal level of Borate in a swimming pool is at 50 ppm. This is also the max recommended level set by both the EPA and NSF International, though the EPA warning is not required to be on the label unless algastat claims are listed. As most state health department codes dictate that only chemicals certified to NSF60 (NSF50 at a minimum for some) are for public pool use, this 50 ppm max in these applications is the law.

You will want to ensure that you utilize a borate test kit to monitor these levels, as you should for anything you add to the pool water when a test kit exists. Residential pools should not be held to a different standard just because they are not regulated.

If your homeowner should decide to fact check you on Google, they may find that studies have found that high levels of borates can cause reproductive issues in animals. Ugh! Is it true? I did not receive an invitation to participate in those studies, so I cannot say first hand, but I believe the research is accurate.

That does not mean that the product is dangerous in moderation. Every chemical we use in a swimming pool has a maximum acceptable level, although not all will prevent a dog from having puppies. The maximum allowed copper level of 1.0 ppm because levels higher than 1.3 ppm in drinking water can be dangerous. Heck, even chlorine has a max part per million with human safety as the concern.

Don't drink the Butt Water!

YES! I said, drinking water. This is where a lot of our acceptable ranges in pool care come from. EPA drinking water standards. Or are at least taken into consideration. Yet, we do not drink copious amounts of pool water, do we? No, no, no! People stick their butts in there, so making efforts to prevent the 'butt water' from entering your mouth is highly recommended. Gross!!!

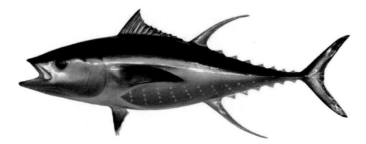

Still, I like to use tuna fish as my analogy. Almost everyone eats or has eaten tuna fish at one point, but we know we are not supposed to eat tuna fish every day, right? Why not? If you said 'High mercury content,' you are letting your genius show. Yet, we continue to eat tuna fish because we understand that it is safe in moderation.

Borates at a level of 50 ppm in a swimming pool, according to the EPA & NSF International, is precisely the same. Realistically, your dog shouldn't be drinking the pool water anyway, and of course, the threat is less for humans because, as we discussed – people shouldn't, and usually don't, drink copious amounts of butt water.

This is the most crucial reason you must own a borate test if you intend to use this product. The other being the health department reg, I mentioned before - you must own a test kit for everything you put into the water for which a test kit exists. There is both an EPA and NSF International regulated top-end level of 50 ppm.

$C_3H_3N_3O_3$

This one sounds like it should be a droid in one of those intergalactic space opera films. You know the one. But, not so much. Here we are discussing Cyanuric Acid. Believe it or not, it is a chemical created by urea's heat degradation—this and melamine. It sounds as if we were better off with the droids.

The Cyanuric Acid compound forms a loose bond with the chlorine in the swimming pool water. This protects the chlorine so that it is not lost quickly due to U.V. degradation from the sunlight. Without Cyanuric Acid present in a swimming pool, you will lose nearly all of the chlorine you have added after just thirty minutes in a pool with an average depth of 4.5 feet in the direct noontime sun.

To ensure that the chlorine remains in the pool long enough to do its job, we add cyanuric acid. However, there is no such thing as a zero-sum game. We must take the good with the bad. I am not going to lie; there is much controversy about what I am about to say, but the truth is that cyanuric acid slows the effectiveness of chlorine; It doesn't bind it. It doesn't lock it, stop it, or keep it from working. It does lessen the efficacy.

As you may have already deduced, too much of a good thing can be bad for you. Same as when my Doctor talks to me about coffee. Hmm. Yes, I am the definition of a coffee addict. Regardless, you should keep the CyA (cyanuric acid) in your swimming pools at the minimum level required to provide the operator with the most consistently beneficial results. Generally, this will be the 30 ppm to 50 ppm but refer to the chart at the beginning of this topic.

Did you know that cyanuric acid use is optional? I have plenty of customers with pools of sizes from 10K to 1M gallons in Florida that do not use cyanuric acid at all. I know, right? They can maintain chlorine levels just fine; however, they go through much larger quantities. Then again, a commercial pool with a heavy bather load can dwarf the 4-8 ppm loss due to sunlight just due to patron use alone. Be aware, much like calcium hardness, the only way to reduce the cyanuric Acid level is to replace water. I have found consistent success in using alum to lower cyanuric acid levels; however, research is ongoing and necessary before I offer this alum-cya removal method as a proven reduction method.

FYI: The pK_a value of cyanuric acid is 6.88, which means this acid, of the acids we use, in the correct concentration, will also help buffer against both an upward and downward drift in pH. I say it only helps because the buffer strength is not near as powerful as Total Alkalinity. However, there is a lag in chlorine's effectiveness due to CyA we need to keep in mind.

Imagine you have an aerial view of a crowd of, say, one hundred people, and they are all milling about. Some have blue umbrellas, open and overhead; some do not have an umbrella at all. As the people walkabout, they continually hand off an umbrella to one another. As twenty-five people leave the crowd, twenty-five new people arrive. The umbrellas stay with the group.

Eventually, everyone has held an umbrella, and everyone has gone without. That includes both those who have come and gone. The ratio is by no means accurate, but the continuous umbrella (CyA) handoff as we lose people (chlorine) to have it replaced by new people (chlorine) provides an interesting visual. The person with an umbrella in hand as chlorine atom bound to cyanuric acid, the person without as hypochlorous acid attached to water. Increasing the number of umbrellas, without an increase in people, results in less hypochlorous acid, which we like to refer to as the 'Killing form' of chlorine.

NOTE: You should only drain water if you are a properly insured and licensed (if required) swimming pool professional with an awareness of groundwater tables and knowledge in the installation of well-points.

Total Dissolved Solids

Total dissolved solids (TDS) is the measure of all particles liquefied in the swimming pool water. This includes everything that came with it from the tap, chemicals you have added, and any crap that has fallen from the sky.

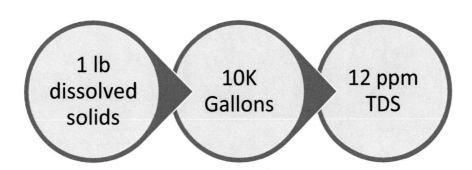

It is essential to understand that anything you add to a pool will increase something, and everything you add will increase TDS. For example, a gallon of sodium hypochlorite (containing 2.34 pounds of solids) will add 12 ppm of FAC (Free Available Chlorine) to 10,000 gallons of water and increase the TDS by 28 ppm. 15 oz. of trichlor (stabilized chlorine tablets/granular) will add 10 ppm of FAC to 10,000g, but it will also increase the CYA (Cyanuric Acid) by 6 ppm and the TDS by 10 ppm. Cal hypo (Calcium Hypochlorite) added at a rate of 20 oz. Per 10,000g will add 10 ppm of FAC and increase your Calcium Hardness by 8 ppm and your Total Dissolved Solids by 15 ppm. Even a cup of muriatic acid (containing 1.87 pounds of solids per gallon) will raise the TDS by 1.4 ppm.

Before you add anything, the fill water straight from the tap has a Total Dissolved Solids level. It is essential in swimming pool maintenance that we know what that starting number is. The TDS level will not decline over time - it only increases, which will require water replacement to rectify. The pool should be drained and refilled by a professional whenever the TDS increases by 1500 ppm over what we started with (except saltwater pools).

If you are not sure what the Total Dissolved Solids level you started with is, test your fill water. H_2O from that location will have the TDS closest to what it was when you first filled it. Levels of anything present in tap water, whether from a municipality or your own well, will vary over time. Still, this is as close as we are going to get until a complete refill.

It is also important to remember that the TDS reading we use is merely an estimate. The meters we use for this measure are electrical conductivity sensors (EC). This is the only practical poolside means. Because we use EC as a means of measurement, this means we only measure those things that hold an electrical charge, like salts and metals.

There are other things in the water that adds to TDS but do not hold a charge. The contribution from those solids will remain unknown. I mentioned I had a coffee problem, so that we can use this as an example. Let's say you, and I have a cup of coffee from the same pot and use the same amount of creamer, except you were to add a spoonful or two of sugar. The Total Dissolved Solids level of your beverage will test the same as mine if we use an electrical conductivity sensor. This is because sucrose does not hold a charge. There will be similar substances in your pool that will also build over time. What a Megillah!

Gravimetric determination is the most accurate method of accounting for everything dissolved in a body of water. We boil off the water and then weigh what is left behind on a scale. This is certainly not the best testing method for a poolside application, and TDS, although included in LSI, is not a significant player. The factor changes only slightly with increases that take years to occur.

NOTE: You should only drain water if you are a properly insured and licensed (if required) swimming pool professional with an awareness of groundwater tables and knowledge in the installation of well-points. Yes - I am going to pound the poop out of this warning.

Phosphates

Some of the industry veterans you'll hear speak and talk about how phosphates in swimming pools wasn't a "thing" until the late nineties. Then all of a sudden, phosphate remover was everywhere. But we maintained swimming pools excellent and with little problem before that. Heck, we even added phosphates to swimming pools on purpose. Wait; what?

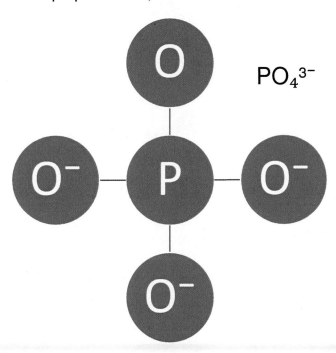

$$PO_4{}^{3-}$$

True story and you are adding it too. The active ingredient in stain preventatives (sequestering agents) for swimming pools was and still is organic phosphates. Yup, and we did this on purpose. Why? The configuration of the atoms in the phosphate is such that the calcium kind of 'fits' inside; it loosely binds to metal ions. It realistically serves as more of a chelating agent.

Some phosphates will form an ionic bond with calcium, magnesium, or metals, which help keep these things in solution when added. So, not all phosphates are evil. The problem is our test kits and phosphate remover products can't tell the difference. So, some would say (okay me. I say this) phosphates aren't a problem until they are a problem.

It is essential to note that Algae doesn't use organic phosphates (the sequestering kind), but these do eventually become a problem. Organic phosphates are easily oxidized over time by chlorine. When this occurs, the result is orthophosphate, which is a vital nutrient for algae.

Aluminum Sulfate

We will speak more on the use of alum (Aluminum sulfate) and its uses in pool water (there are many) later in this handbook. However, this chemical, which is the active ingredient in most products labeled 'Floc,' is also quite proficient in removing phosphates.

Lanthanum

Algae is not very complicated and only needs a few things to grow. Light, phosphorous, nitrogen, carbon dioxide, and water are pretty much all that is on the list. Take one of these away, and you'll put a severe crimp in the success of its growth. Phosphates are the easiest for us to eliminate, which is why it has become the go-to target.

You'll probably not get the level to zero, but it shouldn't be challenging to keep the concentration below the max recommended 100 ppb (parts per billion). Honestly, if you can keep it under 500 ppb, you should be just fine.

The way this works is simple. Remove one of the critical ingredients' algae needs to live, starve the algae. Lanthanum, a heavy metal and the active ingredient in most phosphate removers, binds strongly to phosphate and precipitates it. That is why this is the most common chemical choice. It does the best job of metallic means of phosphate removal. Aluminum sulfate would be a close runner up. The main difference in the application process depends on how and where you wish to clean the mess.

One application collects all of the crap in your media (sand, cartridge, or DE) and requires multiple filter cleanings throughout the process (Lanthanum). The other will settle phosphates and a heck of a lot of different things to the pool floor in a thick sludge that will require a prolonged vacuum to waste. We will talk about alum again, I promise.

As far as phosphate removal goes, I'll leave that up to you. The truth is you will not be doing your customers an injustice if you keep the levels beneath the recommended maximum. If it is part of your specific protocol of care, then, by all means, do it. Phosphate removal is a preventative measure, and it is a service to your customers. Think of it as an insurance policy.

Upon the addition of lanthanum, one lanthanum (+3 charge) binds to one phosphate (-3 charge). So, removal requires a 1:1 ratio of lanthanum to phosphate.

If you don't want to remove them, then don't. As I said earlier, phosphates are not a problem until they are. If you maintain pools just fine at higher levels, I'm not going to suggest you change a thing. However, if you are battling algae and tried everything else there is try, you might want to consider this treatment.

The exception again being a saltwater pool where they have to go, no matter what. Salt cells don't produce enough chlorine to keep up with a phosphate level. That and keep a closer eye on swimming pools at golf courses. It takes a lot of turfgrass fertilization to keep the greens - green, and all that sprayed gobbledygook gets everywhere. You'll see in golf course pools; you may want to treat these whether you believe phosphorous to be problematic or not.

1912 hypochlorite plant in Stillwater, Minnesota. CDC/ Minnesota Department of Health, R.N. Barr Library; Librarians Melissa Rethlefsen and Marie Jones

I don't use chlorine; I have a salt pool

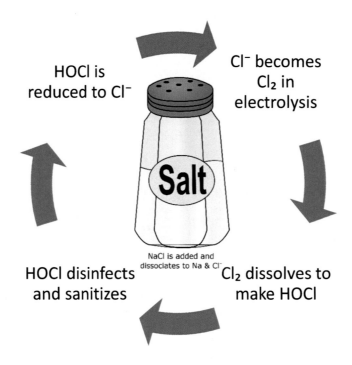

HOCl is reduced to Cl⁻

Cl⁻ becomes Cl₂ in electrolysis

HOCl disinfects and sanitizes

NaCl is added and dissociates to Na & Cl⁻

Cl₂ dissolves to make HOCl

When salt is added to water, we form an aqueous saline solution; the compound NaCl dissociates into Na and Cl⁻. Once separated, the Cl⁻ (Chloride) during electrolysis becomes Chlorine gas (Cl_2).

We add somewhere between 3,000 to 4,000 ppm of salt to a swimming pool (about 250 to 333 lbs per 10,000 gallons) to have enough chloride ions to produce chlorine. Yes, this does also increase the Total Dissolved Solids level (1 pound of salt will increase the TDS of 10,000 gallons of water by 12 ppm). The saltwater solution we created passes through the electrolytic cell containing charged plates, both a cathode and an anode; in this process, a qty of 2 of Cl⁻ becomes Cl_2. Capeesh?

Technically, the saltwater chlorine generator's (SWG) net result is identical to adding sodium hypochlorite except for the extra salt and small amount of sodium hydroxide (lye) in the hypochlorite product. That and the hydrogen gas produced in the cell. So, an SWG cell effectively combines chloride ion and water to produce hydrogen gas and hypochlorite ion. The same hypochlorite ion as with sodium hypochlorite in liquid chlorine bleach. When the hypochlorous acid or hypochlorite ion gets used/consumed, it converts back to chloride ion, so it is "recycled" as the process begins again...

The bubbling off of hydrogen, produced as described above, drives the pH upward by the turbulence it creates.

Bubbles!

Aeration causes turbulence in the water. This agitation then causes the aqueous CO_2 (carbon dioxide) to outgas – outgassing of CO_2 from water results in an increase in pH. Aerating is the only means of increasing pH that will not increase Total Alkalinity. This is both beneficial and problematic.

So, if a water feature causes the pH to rise, it only makes sense that we will need to add acid to lower it. But we just said the Total Alkalinity would not increase due to the agitation caused by that feature. This is a problem. We know it is impossible to add acid to lower the pH without lowering the TA (Total Alkalinity) and vice versa. This means the repeated dose of acid we will need to correct the pH from continuous turbulence will drive the Total Alkalinity further and further into the toilet. It is not uncommon to see that some type of sodium bicarb slurry-feed system for just this reason.

You could use carbon dioxide (CO_2) injection as an alternative to muriatic acid for pH control in this scenario. When injected, carbonic acid (H_2CO_3) forms, and it is very effective at lowering the pH. Unfortunately, the setup is a bit of an expense, which knocks it out of consideration for smaller water bodies. This, and injecting CO_2, will increase the Total Alkalinity. Ultimately, we find ourselves needing to add acid yet again.

I was asked a question just this morning along these lines. So, I thought, why not include it here.

A great question from a caller, who asks, "How do water cannons affect the pH?" With it being Hot Hot Hot across the country this week, this is totally relevant to the time of the season.

Water cannons are popular in pools in the Southeast U.S. A bunch of adjustments in the water chemistry routine may become necessary. I hope you don't find bullets to be rude.

- **Cannons create** turbulence, which causes aqueous CO_2 to outgas, increasing pH
  o Turbulence is the only means of increasing pH that will NOT also increase the Total Alkalinity
- **Pool Operator adds** muriatic acid to lower pH to the acceptable range
  o Acid, no matter how added, lowers both pH and Total Alkalinity
  o Because there was no increase in Total Alkalinity initially, every dose of acid drops this value further.
  o Total Alkalinity becomes impossible to maintain (always extremely low)

Solutions

- **The facility maintains** a lower target Total Alkalinity.
- **The facility adds a Sodium Bicarb** slurry feeder for Total Alkalinity Control.
- **The facility makes the switch** to CO_2 for pH control.

A pretty exciting chain reaction. Even with all of the above in place, on hotter days where cannons are used open through close, it is a massive struggle to keep the pH in balance. Unfortunately, the alternative is a water temp far above that recommended by USA Swimming for competition swim.

Shocking

The only reason we "shock" a pool is to eliminate a combined chlorine level. If you don't have one, you don't need to do it. It's that simple. Sadly, there are not many methods that allow for a direct process of testing combined chlorine (chloramines). The FAS-DPD (Ferrous ammonium sulfate (FAS) - N, N-diethyl-p-phenylenediamine (DPD)) will allow the user to calculate this level through titration (counting the drops necessary to make a color change). A DPD drop test, strips, or photometers can only determine the combined chlorine level, if any, indirectly. To do this, we have to test both the Free Available Chlorine and the Total Chlorine level to see if there is a difference. The difference between the two is the level of combined chlorine. If there is no difference, then there is no combined chlorine level; if there is no combined chlorine level, you don't need to "shock."

This does not mean you cannot super chlorinate to treat an algae problem if you have one or add a bit of granular chlorine to raise the chlorine level when it is low. It just means that a one-time per week maintenance shock may not be necessary for your pool. Maybe it is required. We won't know until we run the tests. It is problematic if you do not shock your pool when it needs it, but it can affect your bottom end if we shock more than is required. We need to look at each pool as unique and lean toward a "personalized pool care" approach, as discussed, versus cookie-cutter tactics.

Did your customer pee in the pool?

Of course, it is essential to remember that shocking a pool may not always fix the chloramine (combined chlorine) problem. Organic chloramines result when chlorine tries to sanitize and disinfect byproducts created during protein metabolism in the human body and released into the pool water in urea. Yuck! These differ from ammonia-based inorganic chloramines; breakpoint chlorination ("Shock") will not remove them. The problem is there is no easy way to know what kind you have. So, when we see we have a combined chlorine level, we shock the pool. If there are still chloramines after a shock, we know they are organic. Ozone, U.V., or sometimes even water replacement is how we rid the pool of these.

If you are interested in doing something every week as a preventative measure when none of the above conditions exist, by all means, do so, a non-chlorine oxidizer (sometimes called non-chlorine shock), such as potassium monopersulfate, will work just fine. Just keep in mind that if we do go that route, this chemical will show up as combined chlorine in tests. There is an additive available that is capable of removing this interference. If your protocol of care involves adding a little extra chlorine each visit on your once-a-week pools, I get it, and I am certainly not going to suggest you change.

First, you are going to need a good quality test kit. You'll want one that can differentiate between Free Chlorine and Total Chlorine, as discussed. If you have one of the two-bottle or five-bottle test kits that you often find at big box DIY centers, they are not going to cut it. These kits use a chemical called OTO to test for chlorine, and they can only measure Total Chlorine. This will not help us, and we cannot use these kits to see if a shock is needed. We may still want to have the test reagent even though we can't use it for the reading that counts, and I'll explain why in a moment.

Using a test kit that comes with either DPD powders (FAS DPD) or DPD reagents is what we need. It's not a complicated or time-consuming process, three bottles at five drops each, then match the colors. Or, count the drops until a color change. Most maintenance techs already have a kit that contains these, but if you are not using that third yellow bottle in the drop test, you are only guessing at the pool's chlorine chemistry needs.

A FAS DPD method will measure smaller increments providing you with more precise measures and greater control of your chlorine chemistry. The FAS DPD titration method of testing *chlorine* does calculate combined chlorine separately.

Combined Chlorine (Chloramines) is a very weak and ineffective form of chlorine that is an irritant and can be a precursor to harmful disinfection byproducts. To tell if it's there, you are going to have to use that third yellow reagent. It will be easy to find in your kit because it is the bottle that is probably still full. Smh.

The 10x rule

I'm confident that this must be what you are expecting at this point. Honestly, I am debating on whether or not I include the '10x rule'. This is the method most are familiar with, stating that to gas off a level of chloramines (combined chlorine), a free chlorine level ten times that combined chlorine level is required. Unfortunately, the calculation contains a mathematical error. In this, the measure for chloramines is mistaken as Nitrogen units. The equation should have chloramines in chlorine units. This error negates the weight factor used in the development of the '10x rule'.

That doesn't mean that the method won't work; it will. However, it does so with an excessive amount of chlorine. It's probably safe to say you can achieve breakpoint by merely adding 'more' chlorine. But, if you must have a multiplier, instead of using 10x (7.6x and with side reactions between 8-10x, giving us 10x), a more realistic factor would be 0.5x (plus side reactions).

Industry Accepted Method of Breakpoint

Even though it is a falsehood, I've decided to include it anyway, but only because it is still widely accepted in the industry and because so many of you will be taking other certification classes as part of your training. With that said, here is the 10x rule that we had refuted above: Multiply the combined chlorine level by 10, subtract your existing FAC (Free Available Chlorine), multiply by your dose (from label instructions), then by your gallonage multiplier. It would look something like this:

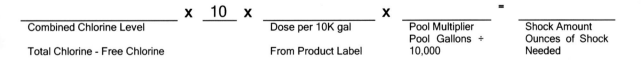

_____ x	10 x	_____ x	_____ =	_____
Combined Chlorine Level		Dose per 10K gal	Pool Multiplier	Shock Amount
			Pool Gallons ÷	Ounces of Shock
Total Chlorine - Free Chlorine		From Product Label	10,000	Needed

Chemical Safety

This is as good as any place I suppose to say a few words about safety. First, let me preface this section by stating that this will not be all-inclusive. Chemical safety goes far beyond what we will talk about, and your attending an OSHA course on such is critical.

In the next section, we will see that even chemicals believed to be harmless can react with one another under certain circumstances. So, think about the potential for problems when dealing with those that are known to be incompatible. This is why we need to exercise extreme care in handling and storing the chemicals we use. I don't want to read about any of you all blowing yourselves up in the News. Got it!?

So, first things first. It is your job to learn which chemicals are compatible with one another and which ones are not. I will, however, give you a head start. Chlorine and any other type of chlorine is a bad combination that could result in a violent reaction. Calcium hypochlorite, if mixed with trichlor, will produce nitrogen trichloride, which can explode. Chlorine and acid is a bad combination that can result in exposure to a deadly chlorine gas cloud. Chemicals and water, let's just say that moisture is not your friend in chemical storage.

Storage Areas

Do Not store chemicals in the pump room. Chemicals should have their own storage area. When stacking products (buckets, etc.), the stacks should be as far apart as the stacks are high. This prevents multiple types of chemicals from coming in contact with one another in a "domino effect" should one of the stacks topple. Better yet, store a pallet of inert material such as sand or diatomaceous earth in-between.

We do not want to store chemicals directly on the ground. At a minimum, on the pallet, they came on. We also do not wish to store liquids above dry chemicals. We already noted that when somethings get wet, a reaction can occur. Also, products like chlorine tend to off-gas. The lids of the containers allow for this to happen. If you have ever been to a pool store, you know this is true. Even though every bucket is sealed, those facilities definitely "smell like a pool store."

Should a liquid leak onto a bucket lid, it may allow a slight amount of moisture in; it could seal the top of the cover so that the bucket cannot pass gas or both. Buckets passing gas, who would have thunk it? Have you ever been to that property where the homeowner leaves their bucket of tabs outside, and it collects that eighth of an inch of rainwater across the lid? If you've ever taken that lid off of the bucket, I bet you that noxious gas that had built up is strong enough to knock you on your ass.

Now, this may sound contradictory, but the type of fire extinguisher you'll want to have in your chemical storage area is an O/S water extinguisher. Wait, what?! Yup, this is precisely what we need here. Some of our buckets, like our trichlor chlorine tablets, for example, have a yellow diamond on the outside with the letters OXY followed by the number 5. This warning tells me that the product is a class 5 Oxidizer, and it will create its own oxygen as it burns. I cannot use an extinguisher designed to snuff out oxygen on a fire that is producing oxygen. It will not work. Our only hope is to drown that fire with copious amounts of water. It doesn't matter how much oxygen it produces; it will not make enough to burn underwater.

A chemical fire adds an extra level of danger. Unless you have undergone the appropriate training to remedy this, you should get your ass out of there and let the fire department handle it. OSHA training courses on Flammable Solids & Flammable Liquids are available.

Dosing Safety

When adding a chemical dose, you'll frequently hear that adding the product to the skimmer, above the gutters, over the main drain, or into a surge pit is standard practice. This may be true, but these are not necessarily the safest options. As long as it is an unpainted plaster pool, I've always been a fan of broadcasting my dose, either dry or diluted. This way, I don't have to worry about what is downline in the system and whether the two chemicals are compatible. Of course, we yield to product label dose instruction.

The exception here being granule cyanuric acid. This stuff takes the better part of a week to dissolve, so tossing it to lay on the pool floor for that amount of time is not the brightest of ideas. Always follow the label instruction for the best method of adding products.

If the pool is vinyl or fiberglass, that doesn't change my opinion, but it decreases our options. We'll now want to look for products made specifically for that vessel type. They will be a little weaker, but they'll be much quicker dissolving.

If you ever need to dilute a product in water before adding it, always add water to the bucket first and then pour in the required chemical dose. Never the other way around. This lessens the amount of dust or fumes kicked up in your face. It also reduces the odds of water catalyzing a chemical reaction.

Calcium and Baking Soda

This pertains directly to the chemicals necessary to adjust two of the values we just discussed in the water chemistry section moments ago. We need to be careful if we ever need to increase both TA (Total Alkalinity) and CH (Calcium Hardness) in a single visit. The chemical we use to increase Total Alkalinity is sodium bicarbonate (baking soda). If we were to add a dose of baking soda and then follow immediately with an amount of calcium chloride (raises the Calcium Hardness level) within too close proximity of one another, a mild chemical reaction could occur. That is why we often suggest waiting a length of time in between additions of these two products. The same holds for sodium carbonate (soda ash) and calcium chloride (oddly enough, this is also an ingredient in store-bought pickles).

I know these two chemicals are known to be inert, and for the most part, this is true. Even if the two came in contact with one another (which they never should if you practice safe chemical handling), a reaction would be doubtful. That is unless it got wet.

Water would be the 'catalyst' in a reaction between sodium bicarbonate and calcium chloride. Four different products would form in this reaction. Some you would notice, some you would not. We would produce salt, water, calcium carbonate, and carbon dioxide as a result. The salt (NaCl) and water (H_2O) made would go unnoticed in the pool. The CO_2 (carbon dioxide) would likely outgas, but it could convert to carbonic acid, potentially lowering the pH.

The calcium carbonate ($CaCO_3$) created in this reaction is a significant problem. You'll end up with milky water as the cloud of powdered "sidewalk chalk" disperses across the pool. The turbidity will take days to weeks to filter out, and you'll have a pissed off customer.

Keep in mind there is a lot of calcium in calcium hypochlorite (shock) too. If added within a proximity of a baking soda (Sodium Bicarbonate) addition, the reaction described above can still occur.

This is just an excellent example of how easy it is for a chemical reaction to occur and how moisture can cause a reaction. If these two 'super-safe' products can react, think about how easily a more catastrophic reaction could occur between chemicals with a more volatile reputation.

SDS and PPE

Don't be a mashugana! Please. Make sure you have an SDS sheet (I know the second "S" in SDS is for "Sheet," social conformity perhaps) for every chemical you have. Whether the product is in your store, at your facility, or in the back of your truck, we need to make sure we have these readily available.

There is a ton of great info on these sheets. They'll cover everything from chemical ingredients to spill procedures. SDS sheets also list the Personal Protective Equipment a person needs to wear in the safe handling of that product. You need to ensure that you and your staff have these items available to them for every chemical. The bright side is that the majority will use the same four or five things, but read it anyway to make sure. Besides, it's the law.

1915 portable emergency hypochlorite plant, packed and ready for shipment.

CDC/ Minnesota Department of Health, R.N. Barr Library; Librarians Melissa Rethlefsen and Marie Jones.

"Whittaker, H.A., Hypochlorite Treatment of Water Supplies; Portable Plant and Field Equipment for it Administration, Public Health Field Reports, 30: 608-18, 1915".

Circulation

I hate dead spots! You did not do this; these things are not your fault, but a wrongly placed return jet will make your life more difficult (Maybe it's your fault. We'll talk in a minute). They are typically due to a design error. Dead spots are areas in the pool that do not have good circulation for one reason or another. It's dead or has stagnant sections. The water in these pockets do not get filtered or chemically treated as often as other parts of the pool.

As I said, this could be due to a design error, meaning that the pool is built wrong. Return jets are in all of the wrong places. Though, it could also be that the returns are simply adjusted incorrectly. This is what we hope for because it is an easy fix. Builder errors are far from easy to compensate for. Wall returns have a threaded collar and an eyeball fitting that allows the pool tech to adjust circulation patterns. You may have to play with these a little to get the best setting, but it is an absolute lifesaver once you do.

Dead Spots Suck!

It is also possible that the pool needs plastering. An old surface can become pitted and riddled with nooks and crannies like the surface of an English muffin. I mentioned this earlier when I was speaking about the Langelier Saturation Index. Water that is not in balance for long periods can have the same result even on fresh plaster. This, in both cases, could create thousands of tiny little dead spots.

Usually, you'll know you have a dead spot because the alga ((singular)(plural = algae)) is going to tell you. If you experience reoccurring algae that begin in the same location over and over again, that spot is probably a dead spot. No matter what you do. No matter how many times you brush it away. Algae will always choose the location in the swimming pool with the most favorable conditions to establish itself. If that is this one spot repeatedly, there is no other explanation. Slow-moving water and a low chlorine level are extremely desirable conditions in a pool for algae to gain a foothold.

Like I said above, this is not your fault if this occurs - unless it is. True story. You didn't build the pool, did you? I mean, unless you screwed up the plaster by ignoring LSI calculations and fail to keep a chlorine level in it, you are probably off the hook. However, it is still your responsibility to determine the cause of the problem and the best protocol to remedy it. Don't forget to manipulate the wall returns like we mentioned to see if that solves the problem. Do understand that if this goes on long enough and you can't figure out how to resolve it, it is now your fault. So, don't let this slide.

Turn Over Time

How many hours a day should the pool pump pump? This is a good question. Unfortunately, there is no one answer, which further supports the need to look at each pool as an individual. That is unless that pool is a public pool, and we will touch upon that in a minute. It also supports my opinion that the person in the field poolside is the best person to make treatment decisions, just as the Doctor bedside in the hospital is the best person to determine that patient's treatment protocol. Sorry, touchy subject. I am not a fan of decisions made in laboratories with tap water in a fish tank guiding regulation for an industry. This is a better talk for another time, but in short, I will put my money on the educated pool professional every time.

First, we need to understand that turnover is NOT the amount of time it takes to filter all of the pool's water. It is the amount of time it takes to filter an amount of water equal to what is in the pool. As it enters through the main drain and skimmers, then back into the pool through the returns, the water is continuously blending and diluting. Because of this, you end up filtering some of the water two and three times before you filter some of it once. Even after four turns, we still fall shy of having filtered it all, but likely by just by a hair.

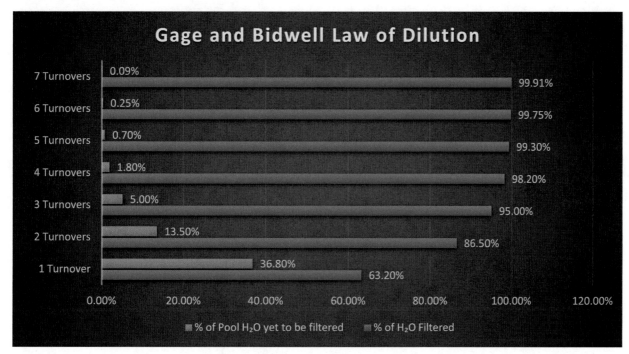

Stephen Dem. Gage, Chairman * †, et al. "SWIMMING POOLS AND OTHER PUBLIC BATHING PLACES," American Journal of Public Health 16, no. 12 (December 1, 1926): pp. 1186-1201.

Here's the thing, there is this 'Gage & Bidwell Law of Dilution' we commonly use in the swimming pool industry to explain the amount of water filtered with each turnover. It accounts for the dilution of water as the water circulates. As you can see, four turnovers get us pretty darned close to 100%. Looking at the chart, I know it's a wonder if we ever get every drop filtered. Geesh! Seven turnovers and still not there yet.

Now, back when I was still knee-high to a heuschrecke, we would size the equipment based upon an eight-hour turnover for residential pools. So, with that eight-hour turn, it would take thirty-two hours of operation to filter nearly all of the water at least one time. Of course, there is no such thing as a perfect pool, is there? I know some pretty badass builders; I bet a few hit the mark, or at least come darn close.

We size for a six-hour turn on a commercial pool unless the local health department regulation calls for the water to filter faster than that. We also run commercial pool pumps twenty-four hours a day in most areas. At six hours each turn, that's four times every twenty-four hours. We are looking to come as close as we can to filtering 100% of the water each day. That is why the health department regulations call for a twenty-four-hour run. Of course, this does not account for any design errors or dead spots. So, the recommended turnover time is again for the perfect pool.

Then we came up with a "Rule of Thumb" for residential pools. Someone said, "Hey, we do not need to run our pumps as much when it's cold out.". Makes sense to me. My left-over schnitzel stays good much much longer in the refrigerator than it does if I had left it out and, on the counter, overnight. The backyard pools would then run one hour per day based upon every ten degrees of air temperature; a ninety-degree day would dictate a nine-hour run time; a fifty-degree day would dictate a five-hour run. This kind of makes sense, right?

Now it is all different again, and the goal is back to one turnover each day for residential, but the pumps are often capable of more than the eight-hour turn. They are larger in most cases, but we program them to run slower, and these we call VSPs (variable speed pumps). A ton of physics comes into play in how these energy-efficient options save the consumer significant amounts of money with only moderate flow rate reductions.

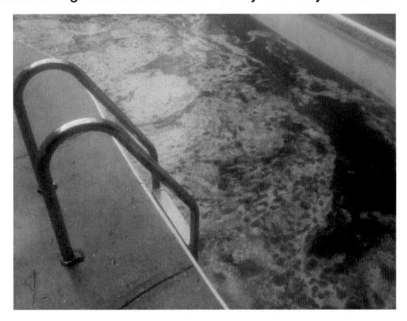

Still, the actual need in a residential pool depends a lot on the quantity and type of debris that gets in it. This, as I said in the beginning, is where we consider the pool to be the individual patient and the Pool Pro to be the primary care physician. You are a specialist; you treat the patients in the field, so somebody should be paying you the big bucks.

With the double aught decade trend of going large, followed by the introduction of variable speed pumps, we have no choice but to calculate the amount of time it takes for a single turn on site.

The formula to calculate the turnover rate is as follows:

Pool Gallons ÷ Flow Rate (GPM) ÷ 60 = Turnover Rate in Hours

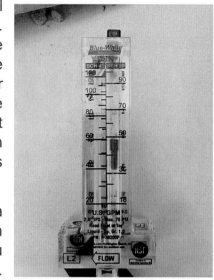

Yes, this calculation requires your knowing the flow rate. Commercial pools must have a flow meter plumb inline, so we are all set for this one. We can pull our GPM (gallons per minute) right from there. The variable speed pumps also tell us the flow rate in gallons per minute, so these also readily provide us with what we need when installed in either application. However, the residential pools that still operate with a single speed pump are where the issue lay. I say, Puffin Schmidt! Why not install the flow meter? It is easy to install and will provide you with invaluable information. Or, better yet - isn't it time to start saving dollars on electric consumption? I'm just saying.

Seriously. I mean, we could calculate Total Dynamic Head and find a vendor sell sheet with a pump curve and backtrack it, but this is a pain in the tuchus when we multiply that process by the number of pools you maintain. Okay, you only have one or two and want to give this a shot. You will need a vacuum gauge reading; I'll assume the filter has a working pressure gauge. The formula is as follows.

$$(PSI \times 2.31) + (Hg \times 1.13) = TDH$$

This is a good number to have because if the pump at a property should ever die, you will need this to size a new one. Unless you replace the pump with an identical brand/model/hp calculating Total Dynamic Head is your only means of measure. Keep in mind; companies do go out of business or models occasionally discontinued. I'm mentioning it now because this is something that you can only calculate with a running pump. Once the motor is dead, it is too late.

NOTE: If there is an existing algae problem, you'll want to run your pump 24/7 until resolved regardless.

Filtration

I'm not going to get into the whole which type is better conversation here. The truth is that a pool can be maintained algae free with any of the filter types or brands available in the market. That is as long as they are correctly sized and properly maintained. Filter sizing is a topic for another handbook, but we can touch on it briefly.

$$Flow\ rate \div Media\ Ability = ft^2\ of\ Filter\ Needed$$

Media ability refers to how much water a filter can handle. For example, diatomaceous earth filters are sized at 2 GPM per square foot of filtering surface area. If I had a 72 GPM flow rate (GPM from Flowmeter with a clean filter) and wanted to size a DE filter to that pool, the formula would be 72 ÷ 2 = 36 square foot minimum of filtering area necessary. Suppose I was looking at cartridge filters for a residential pool. In that case, the media ability is 1 GPM per square foot of filtering area (0.375 GPM in a commercial application). That formula would look like 72 ÷ 1 = 72 square foot minimum of filtering area necessary. Make sense? Just because we don't want to leave anyone out, a sand filter can generally handle between 5 and 15 GPM per square foot of filter area.

If we are sizing everything new right from the start, we always size the pump to the pool and then the filter to the pump. Let me explain. We have a specific turnover rate that we need to hit, whether commercial or residential. The pump determines how fast the water moves (the flow rate). A filter, as stated a moment ago, can only handle so much water so quickly. This we covered in the filter sizing formula. But what if we needed to size a pump to the pool? The following equation will supply us with the flow rate necessary to hit the required turnover rate, and then somebody can size the filter off of that.

Pool Gallons ÷ Turnover Rate ÷ 60 = Flow Rate (GPM)

Backwashing

We want to ensure that we are not overdoing it, but we don't want to underdo it. Not cleaning enough will lead to slow to no water flow, which means nothing is getting filtered from the water and, without getting into the possible equipment issues, will drastically work against us. Okay, maybe not 'nothing' but too dirty will put a severe crimp in our water quality. Cleaning or backwashing too frequently can also be counterproductive. Did you ever hear the saying, "a dirty filter filters better than a clean one."? Not entirely untrue. Dirty Dirty is not what we want, but a little dirty could help us filter out even finer particulate.

Normal Operation (Sand Filter)

Water spreads over and passes through coarse #20 silica sand, through laterals at tank bottom & filtered water returns to the pool.

Backwash (Sand Filter)

Water flow enters backward through the laterals expanding sand into the top of the filter, separating debris & discharges through a waste line.

Every type in every application, the cleaning or backwashing, is based upon eight.

- Vacuum Filter
    - Clean when the vacuum gauge reads higher than 8 Hg (inches mercury)
- Pressure Filter (one gauge)
    - Backwash when pressure gauge increases by 8 psi above starting pressure
- Pressure Filter (two gauges)
    - When pressure between influent and effluent gauges differs by 8 psi
- Regenerative media perlite filter - the exception to the rule.
    - Bump daily (differential pressure not to exceed 15 psi)
    - Change perlite weekly
- Bump Style Diatomaceous Earth (one pressure gauge)
    - Bump when pressure increases by 8 psi above starting pressure.
    - When pressure increases by 8 psi within twenty-four hours of a Bump, flush out D.E. and clean filter.

- Please Follow your filter manufacturer's instructions on the recommended process for backwash or cleaning. Diatomaceous Earth users, please replenish D.E. in the method and dose outlined in your owner's manual.

NOTE: If there is an existing algae problem, you will likely need to backwash or clean your filter frequently due to increases in vacuum or pressure.

Green Algae

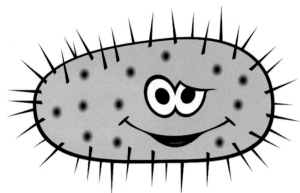

Okay, this should be the easy one, right? Green alga is undoubtedly the most common algae we face in a swimming pool and is the least difficult to eradicate. If you search the internet, you will see that most books, blogs, articles, and sometimes pure propaganda refer to green swimming pool algae as *Chlorophyta,* which is not entirely accurate.

Chlorophyta is primarily a marine (saltwater) alga. Though the class *Chlorophyceae* is predominantly a freshwater species and is in that same phylum. With 2,500 species, Chlorophyceae would be the better name for green algae except for the existence of *Charophyta,* which is a phylum of its own. There are nearly 3,500 species under this umbrella, and it is entirely freshwater though you are more likely to see *Chlorophyceae* than any other class; maybe in this case, "Green" is just the best thing to call it.

How does it get in the pool?

We know algae spores can become airborne, and this primarily how they travel to your pool from a pond (lake, river, stream, swamp, etc.). But how are they getting into the air? Waves crashing to the shore have are the means of jettison on larger bodies of fresh water such as the Great Lakes, Electrostatic attraction to water droplets contained within fog or mist has been known to tote some spores along. Then there is dispersal due to the splashing of rain or precipitation that launches the light sources of tsoris into the air for the wind to carry them away.

Who cares? How do you get rid of it?

Now we have some choices. Just don't pull your punches, and you should be okay. We want to dose with enough of whatever we dose with to kill it. Otherwise, if we are just going to dreck around and piss it off, then you'll spend more money on a second treatment you didn't need, and that'll be aggravating as floc.

Foreclosed Home. Pool untouched for 7 years

Before we can get started, we need to take a few preliminary steps, no matter which route we go.

✓ Remove as much debris from the pool as possible. If the water is so green that you cannot see the bottom, you will need to scoop out what you can - blindly. Do this until there is little to no debris in your net.
  ➢ A vacuum head may not be the best choice as the leaf debris will continually clog the vac head, hose, and pump pot.
    ✓ A self-contained propeller vacuum will not be a good idea at all. The fine particulate can coat the inside of the bag eliminating the suction. This will cause the vacuum head to float or force the bag to pop off, only to be lost somewhere in the pea soup.
  ➢ If the pool is Vinyl or Fiberglass, you will need to be extremely careful not to drag large debris like branches across the pool floor. We do not want to tear or pop a hole in the liner or gouge the fiberglass.
✓ Test your water chemistry
  ➢ Make adjustments to bring the values tested into their acceptable ranges at a minimum, except pH and Total Alkalinity, where we get a bit more specific.
  ➢ Adjust your pH to the lower end of acceptable at 7.2
    ❖ Remember, in the pages before, we discussed the effectiveness of chlorine as pH-dependent, and the lower we adjust it, the more influential the chlorine present will be. Of course, we do not want to take it so low that we drop below the acceptable range.
    ❖ Adjust the Total Alkalinity to between 80 and 100 ppm.

- ❖ Thoroughly brush the walls and floor of the pool with a nylon bristle brush
- ❖ Plan to run your pool pump 24/7 to filter until the water is clear
- ❖ Test your water chemistry

My Pool was Clear Yesterday

How many times have you heard someone say that? I am not typically shy, and I am quick to call bullshit, but could this happen? A bright blue pool realizes a massive bloom going from clean to green in a matter of hours sounds a bit farfetched, ya? Even if it had that hazy blue 'I'm about to bloom' look going on for a day or two - it's not likely we will go completely green overnight. It takes anywhere between three to eight hours for algae to double the population's size, so someone is pulling your leg here.

There will always be a progression. Now, whether the homeowner had noticed this or not is an entirely different story. Thus, the definition of 'yesterday' can often be subjective.

Species of green algae reproduce by cell division, asexual, and sexual means. Are you thinking what I am thinking? That's right; they are in the water making all kinds of algae whoopie. They are photosynthetic, which means they use chlorophyll to perform photosynthesis to produce food. This is with the help of sunlight and made from carbon dioxide and water. They can be planktonic (free-floating) or benthic (adheres to the pool's walls).

This means we are yet again pt into another position where one pool's green algae are not the same green algae as the next. Although easier to remedy, what works quickly in one backyard oasis may not work near as fast in the following – another case made for the "Personalized Pool Treatment" plan.

Chlorine as an Algaecide

Chlorine is a fantastic algaecide when used in a strong enough dose. The accepted industry practice for green algae remediation is 30 ppm of chlorine. In the absence of cyanuric acid, a lower chlorine level may suffice. Maintaining that level for greater than twenty-four hours is typical. Sounds like a lot, right? Remember, if you do not add enough, you'll only prolong the process. How much you add to make this happen depends upon which product you are using.

Note: Jacking a chlorine level up this high in a vinyl or fiberglass pool is not advised.

Doses for the more common chlorine types are as follows.

Chemical Name	Dose	Pool Gallons	Increases Chlorine Level
Sodium Hypochlorite 12%	1 gallon	10,000	12 ppm
Calcium Hypochlorite 73%*	1 lb	10,000	8.7 ppm
Lithium Hypochlorite	1 lb	10,000	4.25

*Calcium Hypochlorite is for unpainted plaster pools only.

How Strong is Chlorine?

Available Chlorine Content (ACC) is probably one of the most confusing concepts to grasp. If you don't get it, don't sweat it. To me, the terminology on the side of a bucket of chlorine seems all upside down and backward anyway. The 'ACC' term compares the bleaching and disinfecting power of the different chlorine compounds. Simplified, ACC is nothing more than comparing that specific chlorine type to chlorine gas and does not have much to do with how much chlorine is in the bucket.

This measurement applies to that chlorine type as a whole, meaning that all chlorine of that type is this strength (or within that specific range of strength) compared to Chlorine gas, which is always 100 percent. Confusing? Okay, the fact that only one of the two chlorine atoms in chlorine gas becomes hypochlorous acid also has a lot to do with it. If we want to know what amount of the chlorine type is actually in the bucket you are purchasing, we will need to look at the listed Percent of Active Strength.

Using standard chlorine tablets, trichloro-s-triazinetrione (Trichlor), as an example. The chemical $(C_3Cl_3N_3O_3)$ is 90% Available Chlorine. This means that Trichlor is 90% as strong as chlorine gas. This applies to ALL Trichlor; ALL Trichlor is 90% ACC (Available Chlorine Content). The 90% listed serving as a comparison of the compounds, as explained above. The product is also listed as being > 99% active strength. This means that greater than 99% of what is in the bucket is trichloro-s-triazinetrione, the amount of the active ingredient.

No, no, Chlorine is not the only way to rid the green. However, because it is the easiest to eliminate, all of the treatments discussed in the following sections, if used in the correct amount, will work.

Historic 1910 photograph depicted a portable emergency hypochlorite plant. CDC/ Minnesota Department of Health, R.N. Barr Library; Librarians Melissa Rethlefsen and Marie Jones.

Mustard Algae

I did a bunch of stuff with black algae; I know most of you are already familiar with those studies. If you are not, I have included excerpts in the pages to follow. Now that you have received a fair warning, mustard algae, like black algae, can also be a royal pain in the tuchus.

Diatoms

Mustard algae can either be dust-like or tenacious, which can sometimes make identification difficult. Some call it "yellow algae," others call it "brown algae," but nearly everyone calls it a pain in the ass. These protists are actually members of the Diatom group, which contains over seventeen thousand species. The same diatoms as diatomaceous earth!

This means that DE could be the fossilized remains of a prehistoric pool problem. Okay, they are not actual fossils because they did not change or decompose. Let's say 'preserved,' as it is a much better description of what had occurred.

Glass Protection

The Diatom's cell wall is made of sodium silicate (Water glass) and does offer quite a bit of chemical resistance. Diatoms do secrete urea, which is pretty gross when you think about it, but this means that urea's secretion can contribute, in a small way, to a swimming pool's combined chlorine level. These tough little yellow nudniks are not only hard to kill, but they make the chlorine less effective and create the need to shock more frequently.

Hint: Diatoms prefer a higher calcium hardness level and slow to no movement of the water. So, we can reduce the possibility of a mushrooming mustard algae colonization by keeping the calcium hardness level on the lower side of acceptable and manipulating our return jets to allow more excellent circulation at the pool floor. Sounds easy enough.

WTF is eating my pool???

Diatoms consume silicates, and swimming pools are a silicate lovers buffet. This does not mean that they do not need phosphorus or nitrates because all algae do. Phosphates are essential for cell energy, nucleic acids, and growth machinery. Nitrogen is necessary for protein and biomass production, nucleotides, and growth machinery as well. In comparison, silicates serve solely for the diatom cell structure.

Unfortunately, we have many silicate sources in a swimming pool; Plaster, cement, diatomaceous earth, and silica sand, to name a few. This may very well be the reason that black algae leave "scars." You've seen this, right? It happens from time to time in pools where the black algae spots have been allowed to sit. I theorize the damage caused by diatoms (mustard algae) that take harbor in the cyanobacteria (black algae) biofilm. Silicate consumption is likely the cause of the blemishes.

Diatoms are the only organism that uses silicates for this purpose - Lucky us (insert eye roll here).

Pro Pool Tip:

If you have a brownish 'dusting' across the pool floor and are unsure if it is mustard algae or sand, we can use the brush test to find the answer. If the brownish schmutz settles back out quickly when hit lightly with a brush, you are dealing with sand. If it takes several hours to a day or two to resettle, it is mustard algae.

Sand on the pool floor beneath the return lines is likely due to a broken lateral if you have a sand filter. Just keep in mind that plenty of other things can cause this, so check them all before you dig.

Note: it takes two times as much chlorine (HOCl) to kill mustard algae as it takes to kill green. If the phosphate level is high, the amount needed to eradicate it will double again.

Just Get Rid of It

Why mess around?? A few folks say vac to waste and then treat with chlorine: one or two others speak of specialty chemicals when asked. Sure, why not? If you have the dusty schmutz type of Mustard algae (keep in mind how many species we said there are), just vacuum it out, boost the chlorine level, and call it a day.

Sodium Bromide

I get asked a lot if sodium bromide for yellow algae works. YES! It does, and this has made this product one of the go-to items for the modern pool tech when the yellow/mustard/brown, whatever you want to call it, invades the pool. But, how exactly does this make the mustard algae go away?

The chlorine in the water oxidizes the sodium bromide upon addition. The result is free bromine (hypobromous acid and hypobromite ions). The existing chlorine bank in the pool water is needed to cause this reaction; otherwise, the bromide salt will not do anything. Bromide ions are lazy, and without a kick in the pants from some type of oxidizer (i.e., chlorine), they'll just sit and watch the algae grow. However, if we can get it to get off its ass and do something, it is a darn fine algaecide.

The main benefit of using bromine is that there is no bonding with cyanuric acid going on here. They are just not attracted to one another. Remember, we spoke about cyanuric acid earlier and discussed how it lessens the efficacy of chlorine? Well, we'll have none of that nonsense here. Just remember, repeated addition of a sodium bromide-based algae treatment in a pool treated with chlorine will result in a bromine pool - until it outgasses, but this takes a bit of time.

This method is not for use with U.V., Ozone, or a saltwater generator swimming pool. Even the U.V. from the sunlight could be problematic and lead to the production of the harmful disinfection byproduct Bromate (BrO_3^-). DPBs, such as this and others, is something we want to avoid.

Cold Pizza and Copper Algaecides

Copper Sulfate is a popular choice by many Pool Pros because it knocks out algae with a "One-Two Punch." Heavy metals lyse (rupture the cell membrane) the algae or bacteria. Basically, it makes it spill its guts.

Copper is also essential to photosynthetic organisms, so algae will readily take this metal when available. However, in large amounts, this metal can prove fatal to the algae. You see, alga is a bit of a glutton, and in the presence of too much copper, it's like the "cold pizza" rule. After a night at the club, you're going to eat a slice, whether you were hungry or not. There is always room for cold pizza.

Copper is necessary to perform photosynthesis, but it will inhibit the process in excess amounts. Without the ability to synthesize food from CO_2(carbon dioxide) and energy from the sun, the algae will not survive. On top of that, copper will inhibit green algae's ability to catalyze nitrogen reduction and cell division in Diatoms. The effect of copper algaecides is immense. They destroy algae and cyanobacteria from both inside and out.

Copper (II) Sulfate pentahydrate crystals Crystal Titan / CC BY-SA (https://creativecommons.org/licenses/by-sa/4.0)

Copper Test Kit

If you are going to start adding copper to the water as either a preventative or an algaecide, you should also own a copper test kit. Honestly, you should own a test kit for anything you put into a swimming pool that a test kit exists for. Like I had mentioned earlier, we follow EPA standards for drinking water here and recognize a maximum acceptable copper level in pool water of 1.0 ppm.

Copper can do a lot of funky things in a pool, so keep this in mind. The water develops brilliant blue or green shades depending upon water chemistry, chlorine level, cyanuric acid, and chlorine addition method. The possibility of cloudy blue exists should there be a spike in Total Alkalinity or pH, and then we should forewarn you of the potential for staining.

Turquoise is a popular color here, but with the addition of a dose of chlorine, you may see the black blotchy staining of cupric oxide appear. Copper may also react with Cyanuric Acid (stabilizer) and form a new compound known as copper-cyanurate. Often referred to as Purple Haze, when this precipitates from the water, a reddish-purple amethyst like crystallization can occur, and you will find it near impossible to remove.

EDTA + Ammonium Sulfate

Disodium salt of ethylenediaminetetraacetic acid dehydrated ammonium sulfate ($C_{10}H_{16}N_2O_8$) WTF?! Okay, but seriously. If you have used Mustard B Gone or Green to Blue (yes, I made those names up. I'm not dropping actual brand names), then you have used this, and you know there are quite a few steps involved.

. Raise your pH to >8.0
. Add 2 lbs of Mustard B Gone per 15,000 gallons of water. Broadcast half and pour the rest around the perimeter *inside the pool* (I have a funny story that goes with this one)
. Immediately Follow behind with an equal dose of chlorine shock (use the appropriate shock for your pool type)
. Run the pump/filter overnight
. Repeat the quantity of chlorine shock

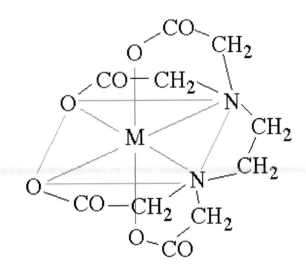

EDTA, Paginazero at Italian Wikipedia / Public domain

Okay. That should be pretty close if not dead on. So, how does this stuff work? We have a bunch of different things that are going on here. EDTA is widely known for its antibacterial properties and was/is commonly used in hospitals as a sanitizer. It is also the active ingredient in one of the big brand names, "chlorine" wipes, yup no chlorine. EDTA is also a chelating agent and reduces "shmear adhesion." Shmear adhesion is what allows black algae and some forms of mustard algae to attach to pool walls. These properties make EDTA both a successful anti-biofilm and an algastat for any 'sticking to the wall' types of algae. On the downside, chlorine oxidizes it quickly, so using a large dose will increase chlorine demand.

But wait, there's more

Here is where the magic happens. As this is a salt of EDTA with ammonium sulfate added, chlorine reacts with it upon addition. When the chlorine attempts to oxidize the ammonium sulfate, the result is the creation of monochloramine instead. Yup, we just created chloramines, and in this case, that's a good thing.

Monochloramine is slower at disinfecting than FAC (Free Available Chlorine), so it's going to last in the pool water a bit longer. NH_2Cl (chloramines) also has no attraction to cyanuric acid, so those bonds in high levels that impede FAC's effectiveness are not a factor here either. As I mentioned above, this product in these combinations provides us with a whole lot of algae, killing goodness. This is why many municipalities use monochloramine to sanitize drinking water.

Obviously, with a pure EDTA (no ammonium sulfate added), the monochloramine creation, as described above, does not occur. Of course, there are only ammonium sulfate products- with these, it is only the chloramine reaction.

I'm having a party on Saturday

This one goes waaaaayyyyy back. It was 1992; I was one year into the pool industry and even had hair. A young pool tot, one might say.

It is a busy day at the water test station. There was a constant line, maybe a dozen deep. A woman approaches and hands me a Ziplock bag full of water (I can't tell you how much I hated water tests in those stupid bags). She tells me her tale of woe in her visits to two other pool stores, spending hundreds of dollars, and a pool that remains swamp-vomit green.

Of course, there was also a sense of urgency because she was *"Having a party on Saturday."* I was a rookie; I had no idea that every customer with a green pool happens to have a Saturday party. It worked too. It made me want to be the hero. The "Algae Buster."

Okay, no screwing around. I have a party to save! I recommend Mustard B Gone (yes, still a fake name). It hadn't failed me yet on a green to clean in my massive twelve-month expertise. I write down all the steps, just as I had explained above. I show her the instructions on the back of the cylindrical container, and as there are a few steps, I go through them with her twice.

The day before the brouhaha

Two days pass and nothing. On the third day, Friday, she enters the store, livid and with a baggie in hand. She waits in line, steaming until she gets to the test station and lets me have it. Her pool is still green. 🗣️ insert lots of yelling here 🗣️ Once she calms down, I ask her to give me a play by play on how she added the product. You'll get more accurate info this way because if you ask questions yes or no questions, you'll quickly find out that people usually lie.

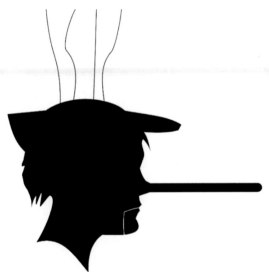

The woman details what she had done, and it matches my instructions to the Tee. I'm scratching my head, and she is turning purple as she speaks. I ask her to repeat the steps. However, this time she adds, "And now what am I supposed to do with all the chemicals on the pool deck?". Seriously?

You see, in my instruction on how to add the Mustard B Gone (step number 2 above), I directed her to broadcast half the dose across the surface of the pool and pour the remainder around the perimeter of the pool. This is precisely what she did. She sprinkled the product ONTO the pool deck AROUND the pool - you know, like the salt circle for protection from evil spirits. WTF???

The portion in purple above has been in my instructions ever since.

White Water Mold (WWM)

Chunks of wet toilet paper floating in the pool. That's probably the most accurate description of what these semi-transparent floating globules of loogie look like. There is not very much information on swimming pool white water mold available anywhere. That just makes treating it all that much more challenging.

What is it? Really

White water mold It is actually a biofilm with the primary constituents being *Saprolegnia* spp. and *Chytridomycota.* So it cannot be mold because mold is in the fungus family, and in this combo, only the chytrids (Chytridomycota) are in the kingdom Fungi. So technically, ½ pathogenic mold and ½ saprotrophic/necrotrophic Eukaryote.

There's a Fungus Among Us

Saprolegnia spp. is in the kingdom *Chromista* and is filamentous, just like actual mold, making it misleading by appearance. *Chytridomycota,* which also has bacteria like properties, is a one-celled organism more similar to an amoeba than anything else. Even the name given to the phylum (*Oomycota*), which *Saprolegnia spp* belongs to, means "Egg Fungus."

Toilet Paper

These glops of translucent gak are parasitic. That means if it is present, there must be some decaying matter somewhere in the system that is serving as an entrée. This also explains why the occurrence is limited primarily to neglected swimming pools. Keep in mind that this does not mean the water needs to be green, just that something is likely to be rotting somewhere. Oy, right in the kishka! I am not insinuating that you or the pool owner are Pig-Tots; no, not at all. These things happen to the best of us. The plumbing or filter could easily be the hiding place for something stuck out of sight beneath the ground, possibly at a ninety-degree PVC elbow fitting, depending on the configuration. But the lack of a chlorine level, okay, that we can call neglect.

What about Pink Algae?

Pink Algae, or sometimes called Pink Slime, is rarer than white water mold. So why bring it up here? Well, I chose to plop it right in the middle of this section because it is all one and the same. Huh? As we mentioned above, WWM (white water mold) is a biofilm, and biofilms will harbor many other things, such as bacteria.

Is it Harmful?

The answer here is YES!!! Let's just, for conversation's sake, assume that anything we refer to as a parasite is terrible. Methyolbacterium is a pathogen and can cause infections, especially in individuals with compromised immune systems. *Saprolegnia* spp and *Chytridomycota* are both considered pathogens, though their typical pathogenic targets are fish and amphibians. Then there are still other things that may take harbor within the biofilm that is scarier than the thought of pooping flaming porcupines. For example, *Legionella spp.* is a bacterium found in biofilms similar to this (white water mold), which can be extremely harmful, even deadly.

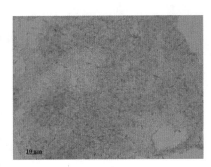

Methyolbacterium is one of those bacteria that often seek protection in the cellulose/glucose schmutz produced by white water mold. It does just happen to turn the white mold pink—the pinker the color, the more **Methylobacterium** taking safe harbor.

Photo: Dr. Sahay / CC BY-SA (https://creativecommons.org/licenses/by-sa/3.0)

The scariest of all pool bacteria

Legionella spp. is a pathogenic group of bacteria found in bodies of freshwater. One of the species included in this group is _L. pneumophilia,_ which is of particular concern. This is the scariest of recreational water bacteria illnesses. IMO

First encountered in the mid-seventies in Philadelphia, members of an American Legion hall had traveled to attend our country's bicentennial event. Over two hundred people would become ill, and many members would die. Because these were the first known cases, the illness name is for the legionnaires who had become sick or had passed.

Raccoon Poop

The only threat scarier, again, in my opinion, is _Baylisascaris procyonis_. This is also known as the raccoon roundworm. It comes from raccoon poop. If your pool has had a visitor in the middle of the night, you may see that one of these vermin have left you a present. It usually can be found on the very top step of the pool, or in the gutter, in the shallowest areas of the water. If the raccoon who has blessed your swimming pool is hosting the roundworm, it can shed upwards of two hundred fifty-thousand eggs per gram of feces.

Unfortunately, there is no treatment for this should the roundworm egg be ingested, hatch, enter the blood stream and find its way to the brain. Now that's a scary animal poop, which has made it number one on my list of frightening pool illnesses. However, this is not associated with WWM.

Where does Legionella come from?

Found naturally in freshwater environments, a poorly maintained swimming pool in a warm climate or spa makes the perfect home for _Legionella pneumophilia_, as do fountains, water towers, A.C. units, etc. Inhaling the bacteria in tiny airborne water droplets dislodged from a contaminated body of water is the method of contraction. A swimming pool is usually not a threat unless it has some type of water feature, but even then, the cooler pool temps help to thwart this. A spa, fountain, or splash pad is a whole different story. Anything that throws water into the air could be a potential concern.

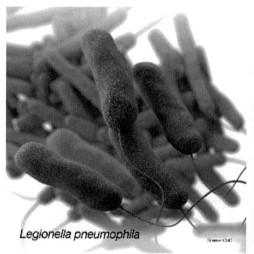

Legionella pneumophila

This illustration depicted a three-dimensional (3D), computer-generated image, of a group of Gram-negative, Legionella pneumophila, bacteria. The artistic recreation was based upon scanning electron microscopic (SEM) imagery. CDC/ Sarah Bailey Cutchin, Illustrator: Dan Higgins

Another thing these non-conventional pool types all have in common is that they are considered high risk. They are smaller bodies of water that we abuse the bejabbers out of, making them more challenging to maintain and, therefore, more likely to have a low sanitizer level. Sadly, _Legionella pneumophilia_ has one of the highest mortality rates of anything we deal with. Even scarier is that because contraction occurs by breathing, you don't even have to get into the water to get it - you need only walk past it during operation.

Lucky for us, *Legionella pneumophilia* cannot survive very long in pool water when its chemistry is within the recommended guidelines. That is unless it has taken harbor in something that can protect it, like WWM.

Back to White Water Mold

Dude... Indeed, WWM occurs more frequently in swimming pools utilizing PHMB (polyhexamethylene biguanide), but it can and does occur in pools that use chlorine as a disinfectant when folks have slacked. PHMB is a polymer disinfectant treatment that includes periodic additions of Hydrogen peroxide (H_2O_2) as an oxidizer. FYI: Chlorine and PHMB do not play well together, so do not add both to the same body of water unless you are specifically looking for a rainbow of vomit colors.

How do we kill White Water Mold?

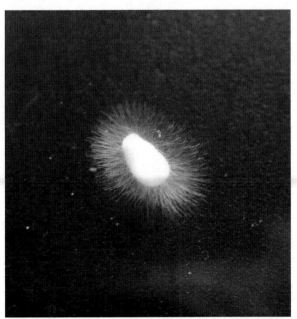

No lie, this stuff can be a sonofabitch to get rid of once it is established. The biofilm slime that the *Saprolegnia* spp. and *Chytridomycota* create contains cellulose, glucans, and chitin. These secretions intended for protection do a fantastic job of making them chlorine resistant.

Photo: No machine-readable author provided. Keisotyo assumed (based on copyright claims). / CC BY-SA (http://creativecommons.org/licenses/by-sa/3.0/)

We will discuss copper sulfate ad nauseam in Mustard Algae eradication (before WWM) and the Black Algae Copper Experiment section ahead, so I do not see a need to revisit that. However, the product is quite successful here, as well. The vital takeaway is that metallic algaecides are incredibly useful at lysing bacteria. There has also been reported success with DBDMH (1,3-dibromo-5,5-dimethyl hydantoin). These tablets only produce hypobromous acid, not the hypobromous acid /hypobromite ion (not compatible with PHMB) combo associated with the Hot tub or pool bromine tablets.

Radiation and O₃

UV radiation and Ozone are the clear winners in WWM remediation. Ozone faring the best when dosed at a rate of 0.50 mg/l. However, this means of oxidation is supplied by installed generators, so some foresight would have been necessary here. I would install one, the other, or both as part of the treatment anyway.

It may add a few days onto the remediation of our floating T.P. snot, but what's a few days if we can ensure that it does not occur again. Of course, nothing is a guarantee, but adding Ozone or UV will make the odds of reoccurrence much less likely. Do remember using Bromine with Ozone, or UV is a big no-no. However, adding a peroxide dose (H_2O_2) in conjunction with one of these supplemental oxidizers will expedite the remediation—kind of like an O₃ or UV steroid.

Advanced Oxidation Process (AOP): In one manner or another (Ozone/UV, Ozone/Hydrogen Peroxide, UV/Hydrogen Peroxide, or Hydrogen Peroxide/Ozone/UV), the hydroxyl radical is the result of the dissociation of hydrogen peroxide (H_2O_2). The product is •OH, which is the neutral form of hydroxide (OH-). Although short-lived, the hydroxyl radical destroys organics and inorganics by breaking them apart (cracking).

Black Algae

Black algae are one of those things we just hope we never get in a pool. It's tough, that is for sure. Probably none tougher. There is also very little known about it. That does not help us any in the treatment process. I'm sure the same as you; I've heard tons of things over the years and had believed many of them to be true. 'It has roots,' 'It embeds in the plaster,' 'You get it when you swim with a suit on that you had used in the ocean,' 'Even if you get rid of black algae, it is like herpes and will keep coming back,' 'The only way to kill it is by draining and acid washing,' 'You might as well fill the pool in with dirt, etc., etc. We all can agree that it is the absolute toughest son of a bitch to get rid of.

In early 2018, I decided that an article on algae would be valuable for my readers at Pool Operator Talk News - www.CPOclass.com. I wanted it to be super accurate; after all, I'm not immune to bad habits and swimming pool folklore myself. I always double and triple-check any information before I put something out there. Even this handbook (originally a pamphlet) is to be reviewed by both a swimming pool water chemistry expert, a Ph.D. specializing in algal physiology and community ecology in aquatic systems, and an industry scientist as my editor before you ever get to see it.

With a scarcity of scientific studies on swimming pool black algae available, I will need to conduct my own research to present you with a complete guide on algae. FYI - when I say scarcity, I mean none. And, I can't just leave black algae out if it's going to be a handbook on how to deal with the funk that can grow in swimming pools. That's why I chose to include white water mold. As rare an occurrence as it is, it still occurs. Understand when I say none, I mean nothing scientific; nothing that documents what black algae are. There are, however, many publications that speak based on hearsay and speculation. Besides, how can we treat this effectively if we don't know what it really is?

To locate samples, I reached out to some of my **students** to see if any had taken on a new pool that possibly had colonization. **Success!** On March 30th of 2018, I gathered several 1/6-ounce screw-cap vials and a 30 ml ampule of Lugol's solution (Yes, I just happen to have these things). I carefully removed samples from the public swimming pool walls by scraping them for placement into the vials. I then added the aqueous iodine for preservation.

Getting Algae into a vial is like trying to catch a fart in a hurricane with a butterfly net

I stopped in to see my friend Professor Phlips Ph. D. of the Phycology Research Lab at the University of

Florida's Center for Aquatic and Invasive Plants with specimens in hand. Dr. Phlips serves as a professor of algal physiology and ecology at the university and is one of the country's foremost experts on algae.

This was and was not surprising

The phycologist confirmed that the dime-sized samples of black algae I had collected were NOT algae. Instead, they were thick matted layers of not one but several genera of cyanobacteria (blue/green algae) in an intertwined colony. *Oscillatoria*, *Microcoleous*, and *Nostoc sp.* were the most prevalent. Understand that this is the only classification by genus, each of which has several hundred species. Of the three genera mentioned, Dr. Phlips found the discovery of *Nostoc* within the thimble-sized clusters to be the most interesting, stating, "*Nostoc* is a nitrogen-fixing cyanobacterium."

Finding nitrogen-fixing bacteria in a swimming pool is pretty cool. That means that this backyard oasis invader could convert atmospheric nitrogen (N_2) into ammonia (NH_3). With an assist from ammonifying bacteria, or by merely grabbing a hydrogen ion (H^+), ammonia (NH_3) quickly becomes ammonium (NH_4^+), which is the predominant type of nitrate algae will use.

This DOES NOT mean that phosphates are not necessary. Phosphorous is essential to all living things and is vital for growth. Lowering the phosphate levels is not likely to kill existing algae or cyanobacteria, but it will slow the growth.

A discovery?

My research was first to document swimming pool 'black algae' as cyanobacteria. My studies were also the first to identify the swimming pool 'black algae' as a biofilm. During my field studies in 2018, there was only one other research document that we could find that refers to cyanobacteria in a swimming pool. It does not tie cyanobacteria to Black Algae, so the determination made was not announced. The study was specific to algaecide effectiveness utilizing field samples of Phormidium *minnesotense* (Family *Oscillatoriaceae*) *and Plectonema sp.*

The Document is titled *Laboratory Comparison of the Effectiveness of Several Algicides on* Isolated *Swimming Pool Algae,* written by R. P. Adamson and M. R. Sommerfeld of the Department of Botany and Microbiology, Arizona State University, Tempe, Arizona 85281, appeared in the Applied and Environmental Microbiology, in February of 1980.

I have since found that the team of R.P. Adamson and M.R. Sommerfield also published *Influence* of *Stabilizer Concentration on Effectiveness of Chlorine as an Algicide* while at Arizona State in December of 1980. Here, chlorine's effectiveness at varying cyanuric acid levels was tested on cyanobacteria but again failed to mention that the Cyanophyta used for the studies are or had come from swimming pool black algae. We also note *Phormidium inundatum Kützing ex Gomont* briefly mentioned as an occurrence in swimming pools in the Encyclopedia of Inland Waters, by J.M. Burkholder, published in 2009. I am sure others may turn up over time.

Does this make our 2018 field studies derivative? Not at all. Had we done nothing more than confirm the presence of cyanobacteria, then maybe. Our research docs are the only studies I am aware of that: identifies black algae as a misnomer for cyanobacteria biofilm, notes the existence of several genera per single colony, investigates toxicity levels, and recognizes 'black algae' as a biofilm where the constituents vary by geographic location in a distance as minimal as one mile. All new information I had brought to the table.

On top of that, we did identify a new genus or two to inhabit chlorinated pool waters. We have also conducted the only known (known, so far

☺) documented non-lab studies of algicides on swimming pool cyanobacteria. One hundred percent of our research occurs in active swimming pool environments, except genera and toxin, which require lab analysis.

Protozoa hiding in the biofilm?

Though we did not test specifically for other harmful pathogens among the cyanobacteria, the U.F. Professor agreed that other bacteria and protozoa are likely to have taken harbor within the mass. We also did not test for the presence of cyanotoxins. However, certain species of *Oscillatoria sp.* and *Nostoc sp.* are known to be toxigenic. Others have been known only to release cyanotoxins upon rupture (lysis) of the cell membrane.

Photosynthetic

One of the unique characteristics of cyanobacteria that set it apart from other bacteria is that it has some plant-like/protist-like features. Specifically, cyanobacteria contain chloroplasts and perform photosynthesis, just as plants/protists do. This means that these microbes utilize sunshine, water, and CO_2 (carbon dioxide) to produce both carbohydrates and oxygen. Scientific American credits cyanobacteria as the "Origin of Oxygen in Earth's Atmosphere." This use of chlorophyll may serve as the prokaryote's Achilles' heel for us as pool professionals.

Heavy Metal!

Here we recognize the benefits of heavy metal. No, James Hetfield of Metallica will not treat 'Black Algae' problems as they arise, though that would be cool. I'm talking copper and silver here. Quaternary algaecides (quaternary ammonium compounds) have reported a smidgeon of success in treating cyanobacteria. Withal, the doses of copper necessary for toxicity would be well over the recommended application rates.

I've had tons of success sprinkling calcium hypochlorite or granular trichlor directly over the colonies (unpainted/unpigmented plaster pools only) or by chalking (rubbing a trichlor tablet on the spots (unpainted/unpigmented plaster pools only) like a stick of sidewalk chalk when and where I could. We even have "Trichlor Tablet Holders" available that enable the **pool operator** to attach a 3" tablet to a telepole for this purpose. Sprinkling granules of trichlor is often more successful than cal hypo due to the lower pH of the product. Watch your metal levels here, the presence of any with chlorine could cause oxidation, and severe staining would occur.

Keep in mind that the sprinkling methods only work with the cyanobacteria that have taken residence on the pool floor. Chalking with the tablet holder makes sense when we have only a handful of small cluster communities on the walls. Neither addresses the pool as a whole, and these methods can only treat what we can see. Remember, both algae and bacteria are microscopic, and you do not see them until there are tens of thousands of them. Scientists who study algae don't always use an actual cell count to measure growth, as it is a tedious process. Instead use a fluorometer to measure the amount of chlorophyll present in a given area is the go-to for an indirect approach.

Use of Copper in Chloroplasts

Here is where copper is pretty badass. Copper is essential to photosynthetic organisms; however, in large amounts, it can prove fatal. We discussed this a bit in our earlier conversations on White Water Mold and Mustard algae. Swimming pool white water mold, if you remember, was also a biofilm.

Copper is necessary to perform photosynthesis. Howbeit, in excess, the metal will inhibit the process. Without the ability to synthesize food from CO_2 (carbon dioxide) and energy from the sun, the bacteria, like any photosynthetic organism, will not survive. Copper will also cause lysis (rupturing of the cell membrane). So, a copper algaecide as a treatment is damaging from both inside and out.

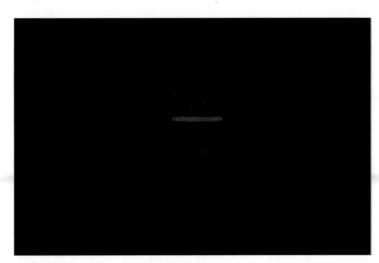

Fig. 7 *Synechococcus* sp. 400X Green-light Epifluorescence

The oligodynamic effect also comes into play

Certain heavy metals kill bacteria and viruses upon contact, and we see that copper has a slightly higher kill rate than silver. Silver ions, however, alter proteins within bacteria, which results in complete inactivation. In systems that utilize both copper and silver, it is the belief that the copper penetrates the cell wall (lysis), providing the silver with an entry point expediting the annihilation.

What exactly happens within a cell in the presence of heavy metals (The oligodynamic effect) is still theorized. Thoughts range from DNA, RNA, enzyme, and cellular protein destruction; to hydroxyl radical formation.

Success in Water Treatment

Ozone, permanganate (commonly used to treat iron bacteria in well water), chlorine, chlorine dioxide, and U.V. are all proven methods of cyanobacteria treatment. Ozone and U.V. work better with a dose of hydrogen peroxide (AOP); oddly, hydrogen peroxide alone doesn't do diddly squat. It is essential to point out that the successes in the results reported involving single cells vs. colonized cyanobacteria have all occurred at drinking water treatment facilities. All of the methods above are dependent upon pH, temperature, and contact time. As I had mentioned previously, scientific studies on swimming pool black algae are minimal.

Iron bacteria oxidizes ferrous iron (solubile) into ferric iron (insolubile) resulting in a slimy brown guck

Black Algae Treatment Field Study

Obviously, with the treatment studies discussed earlier having all occurred in water treatment plants or labs, the next step would be to conduct a treatment study of my own. We have already spoken a bit about copper sulfate as a remedy, but we have a problem.

If this will be a real-world swimming pool test (and it is), we will have to conduct our experiment with less than a lethal dose. I know I sound meshuga, but to be honest, we have no choice. From what we could find in the water treatment industry, heavy metals (copper/silver) would yield the most desirable results. The problem is that every scientific study I could find in the drinking water treatment field indicates that the operator would need a 5.0 ppm level of copper to kill the stuff. In the U.S., we have a maximum allowable level of 1.0 ppm for copper in a swimming pool (0.1 ppm for Silver). Thus "less than a lethal dose." Besides, a level above 1.0 ppm of copper would cause significant staining in a swimming pool that maintained a pH in the ranges that we keep.

A level within the EPA guidelines

I hope to prove that even a non-lethal dose of copper sulfate will prove fatal to cyanobacteria with the increased contact time. With nearly all-available research on copper in cyanobacteria treatment being the result of laboratory studies, I decided to tackle a real-world application. I mean, swimming pools are not laboratory experiments; they are active bodies of water in uncontrolled environments. So, we need a test pool with natural cyanobacteria growth that people swim in and outside in a yard or something.

I know we use copper algaecides all the time, so what would this prove. I get that. My experiment here is that I want to test it out as a 'stand-alone.' I don't want to futz with any of the run times, jack the chlorine level, or adjust any other water chemistry parameters. I want to add the copper sulfate and a strict brushing regimen and leave everything else as is. That's it. See how it does on its own.

Luckily, it did not take long before a facility had offered to allow us to use their swimming pool. But, what we had procured may prove to be a much greater challenge than anticipated. Two hundred thirty thousand gallons (230,000 gals) of water and more than fourteen years (> 14 years) of 'black algae' (cyanobacteria) growth.

The Specifics:

"L" shaped Class A Competition Pool: 230K gallons of water; location: Florida; >14 years of documented Black Algae growth.

Equipment: Qty of 2 of 7.5 hp Baldor pump; field built vacuum D.E. - qty 108 of 19" circular grids - 423.36 sq ft of filter area; 675 GPM flow rate - 5.679-hour turn over; uses sodium hypochlorite 10% to 10.5%; Stenner #45M2 set at max 0.42 gph. Water quality visual: Limpid. Max bather load: 135

Recent Health Inspection Violations

The pool shall be free from floating debris, sediment, dirt, algae. The main drain shall be visible

- Free chlorine level must be between 1-10mg/L (parts per million) in conventional swimming pools, inclusive; or 1½- 10 ppm bromine. Spa pools & IWFs must maintain 2-10 mg/L free chlorine, or 3-10mg/L bromine. The maximum disinfectant level for indoor conventional swimming pools is 5 mg/L chlorine or 6 mg/L bromine. Pool owner must prohibit pool use when water quality is outside these parameters.
- The pH in all pools shall be maintained between 7.2 and 7.8, inclusive. Pool owner must prohibit pool use when water quality is outside these parameters.
- All pools shall have a functional flowmeter capable of reading from 1/2 to 1&1/2 the design flow rate.
- Equipment room shall: have Drainage, ventilation, lighting and be clutter-free

Copper is copper, right?

Well, for the most part, and most available to us that can serve as an algaecide in a swimming pool (meeting standard NSF60) is chelated to prevent the adverse effects of heavy metal in water (i.e., staining, etc.). Of course, no matter what the chemists have done to it, the potential for staining will always exist when using any metallic algaecide.

Day 1, Water Test Results

08:00 hrs August 5th, 2018:

FAC: 3.0 ppm

TAC: 3.0 ppm

pH: 7.7

TA: 90 ppm

CH: 190 ppm

CYA: 0 ppm

Copper: 0 ppm

Water Temp: 86 Deg F

TDS: 1,750 ppm

LSI: -0.01

Without diluting, we added the Copper Sulfate product (14.375 quarts - label instructions) to the swimming pool concentrating most of the algaecide into the diving well. We immediately began brushing the walls and floor with an 18" stainless steel bristle brush. I became immediately aware that it has been a period since I had personally brushed a commercial swimming pool. Ugh. This was kicking my tuchus!

The majority of black algae outbreaks occur in pools where either regular brushing of the walls and floor are not part of the routine maintenance or where the surface (plaster) has deteriorated.

Copper (II) hydroxide [Cu(OH)₂]

A wave of blue washed quickly throughout the pool, much faster than I have witnessed in other copper sulfate additions I have seen. By the time the competition pool's brushing was complete, the pool's water had developed a murky blue haze. Somewhat translucent in the shallow end, but visibility levels were less than allowable in the diving well; we could no longer see the main drain grates.

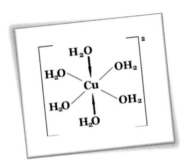

This translucent shade was not the normal hexaaquacopper(II) ion $[Cu(H_2O)6]^{2+}$ bluing experiences that I was expecting. I should have anticipated the impaired visibility due to interaction with bicarbonate ions forming insoluble copper(II) hydroxide $[Cu(OH)_2]$. A pH on the high side and warm water was not my friend today.

I decided to add some muriatic acid to drop the pH to get the cloud to disappear. I need to make sure I make this adjustment slowly to prevent the Cl⁻ from the dissociation of HCl (hydrochloric acid) from reacting with the copper(II) hydroxide $[Cu(OH)_2]$ and forming Copper(II) chloride $(CuCl_2)$. The likely result would be a 230K gallon pool full of Statue of Liberty green water or stained a wicked aquamarine.

12:00 hrs August 5th, 2018

After four hours of filtration, the main drain grates were again visible, and the polyester filter elements had become a brilliant shade of "Infantry" blue. We were now clear and with sufficient time that there would not be a delayed opening. The copper level of the pool water is currently testing at 0.8 ppm.

Where'd all the copper go?

We found the copper level had dropped exceptionally quickly and then leveled at 0.4 ppm for the first week following addition. It then fell to 0.20 during the second week - this due directly to the amount of metal that the algae were taking in. Our tests would only measure what was in the water, not what was consumed by the massive cyanobacteria colonies. I mean, there were 'sheets' of algae the size of high school cafeteria tabletops throughout the pool. This would require a second dose; however, we would need permission from the facility and the existing swimming pool service company before we chance to blue the water again.

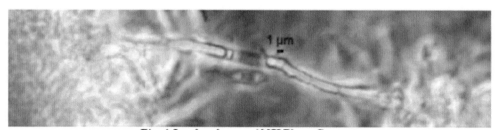

Fig. 4 *Leptlyngbya* sp. 400X Phase Contrast

We received the go-ahead on day 15 and immediately added the maintenance dose of 1 ounce per thousand gallons (7.1875 quarts). We did not repeat 2 ounces per thousand gallons' initial treatment because we already had an established copper bank. The color change associated with the second dose was extremely short-lived.

We know that trace amounts of copper are necessary for photosynthesis and that the process has a reasonably high demand. Cyanobacteria (black algae) must continually uptake metals to support this process. The immediate drop in the copper level from the initial dose was due to the metal's rapid absorption by the massive colonization present in the test pool. This also was not anticipated to be as significant, but as I said, the number of black algae in this pool was insane.

It is important to note that water was not replaced by backwash or otherwise, the test pool does not have a water leveling device, and a substantial leak at this facility is not suspected.

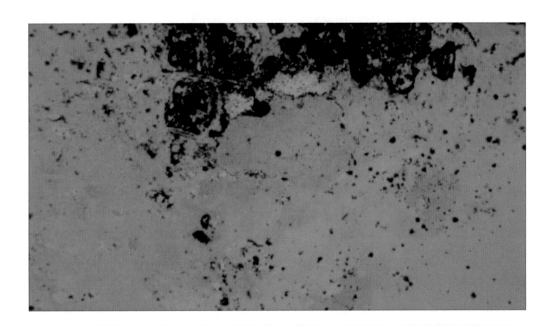

Exopolysaccharidic secretions

I instructed the facilities staff to brush the pool's walls and floors a minimum of one time daily. Cyanobacteria utilize exopolysaccharidic secretions for protection, and for the best chance of eradication, the mosaic protein-**carbohydrate-lipid** "sheath" would need to be compromised.

The first seven days were uneventful, recognizing minimal improvement if any at all. Heading into the second week, the staff at the facility began to note success. However, I cannot honestly say that I could see any visual improvement. Going into the third week following the addition of the copper sulfate pentahydrate, progress would become more noticeable. The algae growth had begun to diminish all about the pool.

Water test results over the three-week period:

	Day 1	Day 2	Day 3	Day 4	Day 6	Day 7	Day 14	Day 16	Day 21
FAC	3.0 ppm	7.5 ppm	5.0 ppm	3.0 ppm	3.0 ppm	1.5 ppm	3.0 ppm	3.0 ppm	10 ppm
TAC	3.0 ppm	7.5 ppm	5.0 ppm	3.0 ppm	3.0 ppm	1.5 ppm	3.0 ppm	3.0 ppm	10 ppm
pH	7.7	7.7	7.4	7.4	7.4	7.4	7.4	7.4	7.6
TA	90 ppm	110 ppm	70 ppm	70 ppm	70 ppm	90 ppm	60 ppm	40 ppm	60 ppm
CH	190 ppm	190 ppm	190 ppm	190 ppm	190 ppm	190 ppm	190 ppm	190 ppm	190ppm
CYA	0 ppm	0 ppm	0 ppm	0 ppm	12:00 PM	0 ppm	0 ppm	0 ppm	0 ppm
Copper	0.8 ppm	0.4 ppm	0.4 ppm	0.4 ppm	0.4 ppm	0.25 ppm	0.20 ppm	0.20 ppm	0.20 ppm
Temp	86 F	88 F	86 F	87 F	88 F	91 F	89 F	91 F	91 F
TDS	1,750ppm	1,750ppm	1,750 ppm	1,750ppm	1,750ppm	1,750ppm	1,750ppm	1,750ppm	1750ppm
LSI	-0.01	0.1	-0.42	-0.41	-0.4	-0.27	-0.46	-0.62	-0.25

Also witnessed during week three of treatment was a fair amount of movement, with portions of the colonies dispersing through "clumping." This is one of the noted waterborne biofilm bacteria activity methods, spreading by literally detaching in clumps. They are also able to move as individual cells through a process known as "swarming."

I could see that we were eliminating the algae, but I wanted something better than 'eyeballing' to gauge how well the process had worked. Through a series of photos taken of a single area within the pool, we assembled a time-lapse video of the research.

We also reached out to Grace Lambert, owner of a graphic design firm, for assistance. Lambert created an image histogram, which would plot the number of pixels in a photo of each shade of color. Utilizing the pixel count, we could then determine the percentage of cyanobacteria in the picture to the picture as a whole.

The histogram results indicate a 50.7414% reduction in cyanobacteria in 28 days of treatment. That is pretty much in line with what we saw - we got rid of about half of it. This is twice the speed it would have taken to achieve a similar result (50% reduction) with an elevated chlorine level and the same brushing regimen.

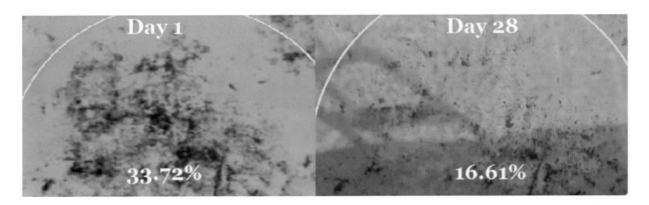

Big whoop de do

I know what you're thinking; still having algae after a month is nothing to write home about. Usually, I'd agree with you. I mean, if a customer had paid me to eliminate an algae problem, you'd be right. But, keep in mind that is not what we were doing here. The sole purpose of this section was as a product test of copper sulfate. Besides, getting rid of seven years out of the fourteen years of growth in twenty-eight days is not too shabby.

Same Algae, Different Bacteria

Alright, so we opened up that can of worms. I found that I may have discovered toxin-producing cyanobacteria growing in Florida swimming pools. I couldn't just leave everybody hanging, plus I wanted to know myself. I mean, since I announced that black algae were cyanobacteria, the phone calls flooded in from other pool pros with concerns of toxins.

I was pretty sure if there were any, the level of chlorine maintained in public/residential swimming pools (minimum acceptable level: *1 mg/L*) will neutralize any toxins produced (or released upon lysing) on contact. But why guess? I'll just find another pool and collect some more specimens.

It didn't take long. One of my students had a recently acquired account (public pool) with 'Black Algae' that she had yet to begin treatment on in the Atlantic Beach area. Colonization was not as established as we had hoped for, but it was more than adequate for specimen collection.

We delivered our new samples to GreenWater Laboratories on October 4th, 2018. GreenWater Laboratories is one of the top research labs in cyanobacteria toxin analysis in the United States.

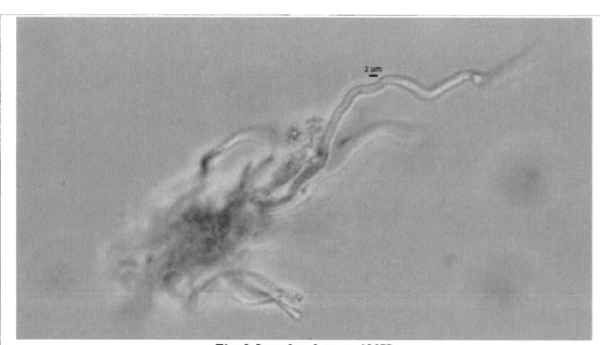

Fig. 3 *Leptolyngbya* sp. 400X

I received the analysis on October 16th, 2018, which was much quicker than anticipated. The information was surprising and added another dimension to our "algae" research. The Atlantic Beach specimens would again confirm that 'black algae' is not algae and that all 'black algae' are not created equal. I mean, there was algae onboard, but that's not what, well, I'll explain in a minute. We did have cyanobacteria again, but it was different cyanobacteria.

The Atlantic Beach samples did not contain *Nostoc sp., Microcoleus,* or *Oscillatoria,* as we had identified in our Gainesville colonies. Our new specimens contain the filamentous cyanobacteria *Leptolyngbya sp.* This was pretty cool and still a noteworthy discovery. The results here evidence that the composition of swimming pool 'black algae' can differ significantly with distance and as little as 100 miles. We have also positively identified several species of true algae that have taken harbor in the cyanobacteria's exopolysaccharidic secretions. This allows us to refer to 'black algae' as a 'Collective Cyanobacteria Community,' a biofilm with cyanobacteria as the dominant constituent.

The makeup difference will be pretty much actual of any algae type, which answers why a certain algae treatment will work in one pool but not in another. Chances are you have something different even though it looks the same; maybe it's not even algae.

Unfortunately, *Leptolyngbya sp.* is a cyanobacterium that is not known to be toxin-producing. I mean suitable for the pool but unfortunate for the test I wanted to conduct. I didn't see any point in spending money on test results that I already knew would be negative, so we let that thought go.

I'm going to need to find cyanobacteria in biomass identical to that found in my initial specimens. Then, depending upon species (300 species of *Nostoc sp. alone* are known to exist), proceed with our analytical work-up from there.

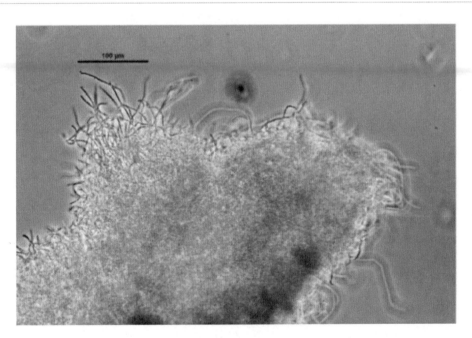

Fig. 1 *Leptolyngbya* sp. 100X (scale bar = 100 μm)

GreenWater Laboratories Qualitative Algal Identification Report: Wet mounts are prepared from the Atlantic Beach Pool sample collected on 10/3/18. Slides were observed at 100X and 400X using a Nikon Eclipse Ti-S Inverted Microscope equipped with phase contrast optics and epifluorescence. The most abundant algae in the sample were species of the filamentous blue-green alga (Cyanobacteria) Leptolyngbya sp.

Toxic Algae?

'A friend once told me that if they were ever to witness my getting into a public pool to collect algae samples, it would be a bit like seeing meteorologist Jim Cantore show up as it starts to rain.'

If geographic location is going to play a factor, and I hope to find results similar to those I had seen in Gainesville, it only makes sense that I look again in Gainesville. Luckily, it didn't take long to locate another. This one was less than one mile from the pool we had taken our initial specimens. This would have to be it, right?

The chlorine level in my sample is a concern

At 10 ppm FAC and Cyanuric Acid > 100 ppm, the level may be high enough to oxidize any toxins present, eliminating proof of their existence, should they exist. Remember that these are not my swimming pools; although I am permitted to collect specimens, altering the chemistry before the collection is not an option. If I were to continue with actual field samples, dealing with disinfectants and algaecides would be among the challenges. Again, the goal is real pools in the real world.

I opted to transport my samples personally (versus shipping) to GreenWater Laboratories (Cyano LAB) in Palatka, FL. I completed the necessary chain of custody form and approved the Potentially Toxigenic (PTOX) Cyanobacteria Screen. Approval for analysis of biomass for toxins would have to wait until the cyanobacteria screen itself was complete. We would again need to confirm cyanobacteria and type to know which toxin tests to conduct.

Andrew Chapman, M.S. of GreenWater Laboratories, contacted me with our cyanobacteria screen results on November 7th, 2018. Again, we would see three different genera of cyanobacteria, and also, our findings would be slightly different from the last two analyses that we conducted. This time, however, as in the first analysis, we observed potential toxin-producing genera.

Does this mean that all pools that have 'black algae' are toxic? Not at all. We have already found that the makeup of black algae is different from pool to pool. Then on top of that, we use chlorine in pools, and chlorine can be pretty badass. The EPA's Cyanobacteria and Cyanotoxins: Information for Drinking Water Systems guideline backs that up, stating that chlorine quickly destroys **cyanotoxins**.

As we had seen in our Atlantic Beach specimens, *Leptolyngbya sp.* dominated the biomass. However, this time in our November 2018 sample, we would again have the cyanobacteria *Oscillatoria sp,* accompanied by a lesser amount of *Synechococcus sp.*

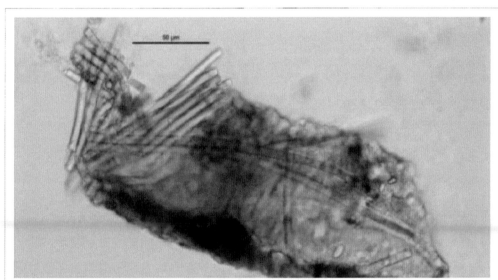

Fig. 6 *Oscillatoria* sp. 400X

GreenWater Laboratories method for analysis: Wet mounts were prepared and scanned at 100X for the presence of potentially toxigenic (PTOX) cyanobacteria using a Nikon Eclipse Ti-S Inverted Microscope equipped with phase-contrast optics and epifluorescence. Higher magnification was necessary for identification and micrographs.

Authorization for testing samples for **cyanotoxins** on November 7th of 2018, but there would be some challenges.

CYANOTOXIN RESULTS

Due to the chlorine level in our sample, testing the pool water for **cyanotoxin** would be futile. If the *Oscillatoria sp.* found in our black algae specimens were actually toxin excreting, the disinfectant (even at the low end of the acceptable range: 1 ppm) would oxidize the hepatotoxins upon production (further testing required). This does not mean we cannot test our specimens for toxins, only that we would be unable to verify a residual.

As we had mentioned previously, cyanobacteria extricate toxins in one of two methods. Either the prokaryote generates toxins, or it releases toxins when lysed (cell membrane is ruptured). Though the swimming pool water chemistry will thwart efforts to confirm cyanotoxin's continuous excretion, we may still detect if toxins release due to lysis.

GreenWater Laboratories
205 Zeagler Drive
Suite 302
Palatka FL 32177
Ph (386) 328-0882
Fax (386) 328-9646

Contact:
markaubel@greenwaterlab.com
amandafoss@greenwaterlab.com

Aquatic Facility Training & Consultants								
MICROCYSTIN RESULTS								

Tested on: 11/9/2018
Method: Enzyme-Linked Immuno Sorbent Assay (ELISA)
Analyte: Microcystins/Nodularins
Analyzed by: Kamil Cieslik

Sample ID/ Date Collected	Initial Conc. Factor	Dilution Ratio	Assay Value, ng/mL	Final Dilution Factor	Avg. LFB Recovery	Avg. LFSM Recovery	Final Concentration (ng/mL)	Average (ng/mL)
Black Algae	1x	none	0.08	1	91%	100%	<0.15	ND
11/1/2018	1x	none	0.07	1			<0.15	

ND = Not detected above LOD/LOQ
LOD/LOQ = 0.15 ng/mL
LFB = 1.0 ng/mL MCLR
LFSM = 1.0 ng/mL MCLR

Submitted by: *Amanda Foss*
Amanda Foss, M.S.
Date: 11/9/2018

Submitted to: Rudy Stankowitz
Aquatic Facility Training & Consultants

Gainesville, FL 32618
(352) 598-0229
rudy@pooloperatorcourse.com

The Assay value of our test results (above) shows that a certain level of microcystin (a specific cyanotoxin) released when lysed. However, at 0.08 ng/mL (parts per billion), the level detected by the ELISA in our samples is much lower than the benchmark of 0.15 ppb (shown). Then consider the 10,000 gallons plus of a swimming pool that would dilute this level. The amount recognized is also far below the EPA Drinking Water Health Advisory (H.A.) maximum recommended level of 1.6 micrograms per liter (ppb). So, to sum it up. Toxins are present but nowhere near a harmful amount in the sample I tested.

Aluminum Sulfate (Al$_2$O$_{12}$S$_3$)

Back to the beginning of water treatment. At least close to it. Somewhere around 1500 BC, references to this product exist in writings in both Egypt and Rome. From that point, we have documentation all along of its use in making water potable ever since. I'm not sure how long the chemical was in use in water treatment before 1500 BC, but I'm sure that it was; that just happens to be the first time someone had written it down. On a wall in Hieroglyphics, in a pyramid, maybe?

Aluminum sulfate crystals, Public Domain, https://commons.wikimedia.org/w/index.php?curid=184669

The use of this coagulant is widespread in society today. Its applications include lake and pond treatment, cosmetics, a blood coagulant in hospitals, fire extinguishers, and is even used as an ingredient in pickles. Coagulation with Al$_2$O$_{12}$S$_3$ is one of the first steps a municipality typically uses in treating the drinking water that comes out of the faucet in your kitchen.

NOTE: Not to be used in pools with pigmented plaster. There are advisories from some salt cell manufacturers about high sulfate levels (check your owner's manual before proceeding).

Okay, so what the Floc?

How is this going to help me? Well, first off, Alum is a coagulant, not a floc, even though it is the active ingredient in most products labeled "Floc" in the pool industry. Why? First, we have already had several examples in this handbook that we call something other than it is. Besides, calling something a "Coag" just doesn't sound as cool.

A floc (flocculant) refers to a product that clarifies water using polymers. Much like water clarifier named products, you know the jugs of blue liquid stuff. That's a floc, but we call it a clarifier. $Al_2O_{12}S_3$ works by destabilizing colloidal particles, making it a coagulant, even though we call it a floc. This is primarily because the pool industry distinguishes flocs from coagulants by the 'settle to the floor' vs. 'filters out' distinction.

Do you know how two magnets push one another apart? Debris, with a like charge, do the same. Alum takes that move apart power away. We then see the formation of metallic hydroxide, which causes the debris to settle at the pool bottom. It looks like a thick sludge—kind of gross. The results are a "Currahee!" moment for sure, but this is not a process you should take on unless you are fully prepared to do so.

The success of $Al_2O_{12}S_3$ is both pH and temperature-dependent, and the sludge it creates will require a vac pump with sufficient suction. I would advise not to tackle this without a professional portable vac system. I don't care how powerful the homeowner's equipment is; I suggest you use your own. I've made it sound like a pain in the ass. The truth is, if you follow the steps, this chemical can be a lifesaver. If you don't and wing it, you may end up hating life.

Green to Clean

Probably the best-known use for aluminum sulfate in the pool industry is in the "Green to Clean." Not the "I neglected my pool for a month, and now I am having a party on Saturday" Green to Clean. No, not that. And not the Coral Seas Green to Clean product that is AMMONIUM sulfate. I'm talking about the REO property, foreclosed home; this pool hasn't been touched in at least two years, hoping I don't find a body in this, Green to Clean. A real swamp vomit green extravaganza.

This is where this coagulant shines, and the efforts in preparation seem minimal compared to the results when used correctly. Yes, there are other ways to do this, and I'm not saying that you should abandon those because there will be times they will still be needed. However, I'm sure you may have picked up on the fact that I don't like to drain a pool unless I have to, and if you are not a pool professional with knowledge of both well points and groundwater tables, you shouldn't be draining anything at all.

Some say a high pH, and some say a low pH. The truth is that this chemical will work at any pH within our acceptable range of 7.2 to 7.8. It will work well at a pH as low as 6.0, but dropping your pH that low isn't particularly suitable for the pool. So, we stick with numbers in our acceptable range. I can tell you this; it will still work at a higher pH, but it will take more product and a more extended amount of time to achieve the same results. For me, pH is always at 7.2 for an Alum treatment.

The temperature is also huge. Too cold, and it won't work so well. Ideally, we want a temperature between 70°F to 90°F. Keeping the Total Alkalinity at the higher end of the ideal range is also advised. Overdosing is also not recommended. Floccing is not a "The more, the better" type of product. We will want a pool without a substantial amount of large debris (twigs, sticks, leaf piles) on the floor. This method will require a slow vacuum to waste (Follow local EPA and DOH guidelines for discharge of swimming pool wastewater), and heavy debris will make vacuuming a hassle with frequent clogging.

Once it's broke, it's broken. If you stir it up, it is not likely to settle back out on its own. So, if you choose to pursue this route, scooping out everything you can blindly before you begin is highly recommended. For you all, with vinyl or fiberglass pools, you need to be extremely careful in debris removal not to gouge or tear the pool surface.

If it does break and stays in suspension, you can try adding an actual flocculent. Yes, a water clarifier. This may help, but no promises.

Filter Prep
If the system has a cartridge filter, remove the element and reassemble the filter without it. If the system has a sand or diatomaceous earth filter, maneuver the multiport valve handle position to "recirculate." This will allow the water to bypass the filter entirely, and that is precisely what we want to do. Running water treated with a coagulant through the filter before the process is complete will likely destroy the media resulting in necessary replacement. So, don't do that.

Add your dose according to label instructions for your pool size, set the timer to allow the system to recirculate for two hours, and then turn off. This is easy to do with the time clock that is most likely already in place. If the pump is inoperable, we can dilute the alum dose with copious amounts of water and pour it directly into and about the pool.

Return after a minimum of twelve hours, and you should see that all of the debris has settled to the pool's floor and is ready to be removed by a SLOW vacuum to waste. The water should be fairly translucent at this point. If you would like to expedite clarity, we can add a flocculent if you want. However, it is not necessary as two to three days of filtration should suffice.

Following the vac to waste, we can reassemble our filter system and resume regular operation. DO NOT leave the aluminum hydroxide (metallic sludge) sitting on the floor for an extended period - it has an extremely low pH. You'll want to vac to waste 12 - 14 hours after addition.

But wait, there's more

Some other things had occurred when we dosed the pool with this chemical that we may have missed in the past because we weren't looking for them. These side benefits may even have you thinking about treating a pool with transparent, limpid water with alum ($Al_2O_{12}S_3$) from time to time. But why would you want to?

$Al_2O_{12}S_3$, when added in the manner described above, is

- An effective phosphate remover
- Removes staining from copper (dependent upon the age of stain)
- Lowers Cyanuric Acid
- Kills algae

Yes, believe it or not, these things are real. This coagulant removes phosphates almost as well as Lanthanum. Aluminum is more reactive than copper, so it also has some success in removing stains from that metal. We also have success using this coagulant to reduce cyanuric acid and the treatment of black algae.

You're going to need a Test Kit

The EPA has an action level for copper in drinking water at 1.3 ppm. So, in the pool industry, we draw the line at 1.0 ppm. For silver, the maximum acceptable amount in most areas is 0.10 ppm. Aluminum is no different. This metal has an EPA SMCL (Secondary Standard Contaminant Level) of 0.2 ppm, so you will need to have an after-treatment residual of 0.2 ppm or less. A test kit needs to be on hand for everything you put into a pool that a test kit exists for.

Your area's levels may be lower than this for pool use - consult your local Health Department for regulations specific to your location before you begin.

Algae Prevention and Eradication Specialist Certification

You have purchased the book. Take the class and earn your Algae Prevention and Eradication Specialist Certificate.

This online class will take you through each of the book chapters, covering the identification of algae precursors, prevention methods, and remediation. The course is conducted in a manner that engages the student, uses 'Real World' swimming pool algae problems that students can easily relate to, and incorporates a format that provides a unique and FUN learning experience.

Are you looking for a marketable point of difference that can give you the edge over your competition? Let's face it; the swimming pool service market is hugely oversaturated. Why be a fish in an ocean full of fish when you can be a Shark? Be different and unique – these are the things that help a customer chose one business over another.

Let your existing customers and potential clientele know that you have taken a course that affords the tools and knowledge necessary to keep their swimming pools algae free. You are the **Algae Prevention and Eradication Specialist!**

Take the class, pass the open book test, and receive your Certificate!

To learn more about the Algae Prevention and Eradication Specialist Certification program, or to register to take the class, visit us at

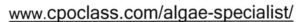

www.cpoclass.com/algae-specialist/

Wrap up

I know, maybe I included a little bit more than was necessary here, but I believe understanding the "why" behind things sometimes make concepts easier to grasp. Then, in this one specifically, if you were going to fight, wouldn't you want to know precisely who or what you are up against?

A swimming pool is a very unnatural thing. A body of water without an ecosystem does not exist unless we make it exist. Then we have the task of delicately balancing chemicals not to damage the pool and its equipment, and we kill pretty much everything that gets in the water (except for the people).

We are involved in a constant battle against nature, who wants nothing more than to encroach on a backyard oasis. Whether it is Algae (as we discuss in this one), viruses, bacteria, frogs, snakes, turtles, or even the whole lot, nature is looking to gain control. Just keep in mind some of the most straight forward actions can have some of the most significant effects.

- Keep your water chemistry readings within the recommended guidelines

- Keep the pool free of debris

- Brush the pool walls and floor on a routine basis.

- Move Planters far away from the edge of the pool

- Run your pump long enough to get the desired turnover rate

- **ALWAYS FOLLOW** product label instructions

- Read the SDS for every chemical you use

- Ensure you are wearing the SDS recommended PPE before handling the chemical.

- Ensure proper operation, maintenance, and condition of your filter equipment

- Always maintain at least the minimum free chlorine level and a pH of < 7.5, but not lower than 7.2

- Have all bathers shower before entering the pool

- Take the time to learn each pool and treat each pool as an individual

- Always be aware of environmental factors that can dictate your protocol of care at each location

Thank you so much for picking up a copy of The How to Get Rid of & Prevent Algae Handbook. I hope to share at least one new thing in these pages that will make your life easier, your pools safer, your company more profitable, and your customers happy.

Like we mentioned going into this, I know this is not every possible method. Some of the pros out there have some tricks up their sleeves that would leave both you and me in awe, I am sure. Drop me a line and let me know. You can find me almost everywhere social media-wise at @CPOclass or on the web at www.CPOclass.com

If you happen to be a pool owner who has received a copy of this guide, it is my strong recommendation to contact a pool professional. I wrote this with the assumption of a certain level of reader experience and an existing vocational knowledge base. The steps within this guide are not DIY, and you should not attempt them at home.

Thank you for Reading
and Helping to keep
Swimming pools Safe and
Algae free!

- Rudy -

Index

References

"The Seaweed Site: Information on Marine Algae." *Seaweed.ie :: Chlorophyta*, www.seaweed.ie/algae/chlorophyta.php.

"Chlorophyceae: Occurrence, Characteristics and Classification." Biology Discussion, 24 Aug. 2016, www.biologydiscussion.com/algae/chlorophyceae-occurrence-characteristics-and-classification/46781.

CARSON2 , Johnny L, and R. MALCOLM Brown. *"The Correlation of Soil Algae, Airborne Algae, and Fern Spores with Meteorological Conditions on the Island of Hawaii ."* University of Hawaii, Pacific Science , 1976, scholarspace.manoa.hawaii.edu/bitstream/10125/10779/1/v30n2-197-205.pdf.

"Legionnaires Disease Cause and Spread." *Centers for Disease Control and Prevention*, Centers for Disease Control and Prevention, 15 Jan. 2020, www.cdc.gov/legionella/about/causes-transmission.html.

"Bronopol." *National Center for Biotechnology Information. PubChem Compound Database*, U.S. National Library of Medicine, pubchem.ncbi.nlm.nih.gov/compound/bronopol.

"Oomycota." *Microbewiki*, microbewiki.kenyon.edu/index.php/Oomycota.

O'Rourke , Dorcas P, and Matthew D Rosenbaum. "Saprolegnia." *Saprolegnia - an Overview | ScienceDirect Topics*, 2015, www.sciencedirect.com/topics/veterinary-science-and-veterinary-medicine/saprolegnia.

M. Gunnar Andersson, Lage Cerenius
"Pumilio Homologue from Saprolegnia parasitica Specifically Expressed in Undifferentiated Spore Cysts"
Eukaryotic Cell Feb 2002, 1 (1) 105-111; **DOI:** 10.1128/EC.1.1.105-111.2002

Parrs, Ronald. "Pink Slime in Swimming Pools." *Ezine Articles*, 2008, ezinearticles.com/?Pink-Slime-in-Swimming-Pools&id=1302592.

MITCHELL , C. "What Is Water Mold? ." *WiseGEEK*, Conjecture Corporation, 2020, www.wisegeek.com/what-is-water-mold.htm.

"Introduction to Cyanobacteria." *Introduction to the Cyanobacteria*, www.ucmp.berkeley.edu/bacteria/cyanointro.html.

Lakna. "Difference Between Prokaryotic and Eukaryotic Cells: Structure, Characteristics, Comparison." *Pediaa.Com*, 25 Feb. 2017, pediaa.com/difference-between-prokaryotic-and-eukaryotic-cells/.

Hoiczyk, E, and A Hansel. "Cyanobacterial Cell Walls: News from an Unusual Prokaryotic Envelope." *Journal of Bacteriology*, American Society for Microbiology, Mar. 2000, www.ncbi.nlm.nih.gov/pmc/articles/PMC94402/.

Varkey, A.J. "Antibacterial Properties of Some Metals and Alloys in Combating Coliforms in Contaminated Water." *Scientific Research and Essays*, vol. 5, 2010, pp. 3834–3839.

D'Anglada, Lesley V, and Jamie Strong. "Drinking Water Health Advisory for the Cyanobacterial Microcystin Toxins ." *Epa.gov*, 2015, www.epa.gov/sites/production/files/2017-06/documents/microcystins-report-2015.pdf.

Arvind Patil, Ph.D., CWS-I Gary Hatch, Ph.D. Charles Michaud, CWS-VI Mark Brotman, CWS-VI P. Regunathan, Ph.D. Rebecca Tallon, P.E. Richard Andrew Shannon Murphy Steve VerStrat Pauli Undesser, M.S., CWS-VI Kimberly Redden, CWS-VI.   "Aluminum Fact Sheet." *Water Quality Association*, 2013, www.wqa.org/Portals/0/Technical/Technical%20Fact%20Sheets/2014_Aluminum.pdf.

Huertas MJ, López-Maury L, Giner-Lamia J, Sánchez-Riego AM, Florencio FJ. *"Metals in Cyanobacteria: Analysis of the Copper, Nickel, Cobalt, and Arsenic Homeostasis Mechanisms."* Meeks JC, Haselkorn R, eds. *Life*. 2014;4(4):865-886. doi:10.3390/life4040865.

"Understanding Biofilms", by Amy Proal, Bacteriality: exploring chronic decease, 2008

P T Srinivasan1 , T Viraraghavan, and K S Subramanian2 1 *"Aluminium in drinking water: An overview* "Faculty of Engineering, University of Regina, Regina, Canada S4S OA2 2Environmental Health Directorate, Health Canada, Ottawa, Ontario, Canada K1A OL2 https://sswm.info/sites/default/files/reference_attachments/SRINIVASAN%201999%20Aluminium%20in%20Drinking%20Water%20-%20An%20Overview.pdf

Spaulding, Sarah. "Do Diatoms Form Fossils?" *Diatoms of North America*, 10 Jan. 2017, diatoms.org/news/do-diatoms-form-fossils.

Special Thanks to the following individuals:

Professor Ed Phlips, Ph.D., UF Phycology Dept

Susan Badylak, Senior Biological Scientist, Department of Fisheries and Aquatic Sciences, University of Florida

Thomas Race, Aqua-Caribbean Swimming Pool Service, Gainesville, Fl www.aqua-caribbean.com

Eli Ben-Shoshan (eli@benshoshan.com) drone footage.

Grace Lambert www.facebook.com/truleeyours/ Histogram Results

Lisa Arquilla Dodge of Pool Care Pros, Jacksonville Florida

Dr. Fred Singleton & Doug McKenzie of Earth Science Laboratories

Mark Aubel and the team at GreenWater laboratories

John Poma of A+ Pool Service, Lakeland Florida - efforts in proving the Stankowitz/Poma Alum-CyA theory

Notes

Notes

Made in the USA
Las Vegas, NV
22 April 2024

89013635R00057